MY FIRST WORKBOOK OF
100 SIGHT WORDS
PRACTICE WORKSHEETS

Tons of practice exercises to help your child read common high-frequency words by sight and acquire this endlessly rewarding skill in a few weeks with regular practice.

By Shobha

Table of Contents

What are sight words and why should it be used?

Sight words are high frequency words that make up for more than 50% of words your child would encounter while beginning to read. It's a great tool for reading as it enhances a child's speed, fluency and reading comprehension.

Sight words are an important tool for learning to read and because they are used so frequently it is important that your child is able to recognize these words on sight (hence called "sight words") without having to use any strategy to decode. There are many words - like "the" - that cannot be easily illustrated. The word "the" is both a definite article and an adverb. It will be very difficult for a beginner to decipher the usage so it's better if they start learning piecemeal – first recognizing the word and as they grow, decoding the usage of the word per the context.

Sight words are as important to learn reading as math facts are to learn elementary math. When kids master sight words their memory automatically brings the sound and meaning of the word into their consciousness. The action is so unconscious that they don't even realize it is happening. Mastering sight words develops automaticity while reading.

Automaticity is the ability to do things without occupying the mind with the low level details that are required; this is usually the result of consistent learning, repetition, and practice. For instance, an experienced cyclist does not have to concentrate on turning the pedals, balancing, and holding on to the handlebars. Instead, those processes are automatic and the cyclist can concentrate on watching the road, the traffic, and other surroundings.

Sight words also build confidence in a child. The frequency of occurrence of these words are so high that a child who has mastered these words can already recognize at least half of a sentence and start to feel good and confident about reading.

Sight words also help promote reading comprehension. When your child opens their book for the first time, instead of trying to decipher what all of the words mean, they can shift their attention to focus on those words they are not familiar with. They will already know at least half of the words, so focusing on the other half helps strengthen their understanding of the text.

Aligns to
Common Core Standard
CCSS.ELA-LITERACY.RF.K.3.C

Other books from the author that might interest you:

LETTER TRACING BOOKS

TIME TELLING BOOKS

BASIC MATH FACTS BOOKS

 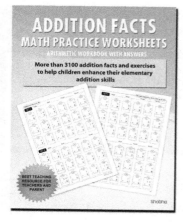 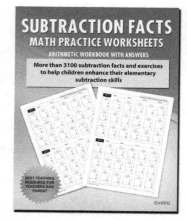 

the

Trace the word as shown and speak it out loud:

the the the the the

Practice writing the word yourself.

Color the clouds containing the sight word:

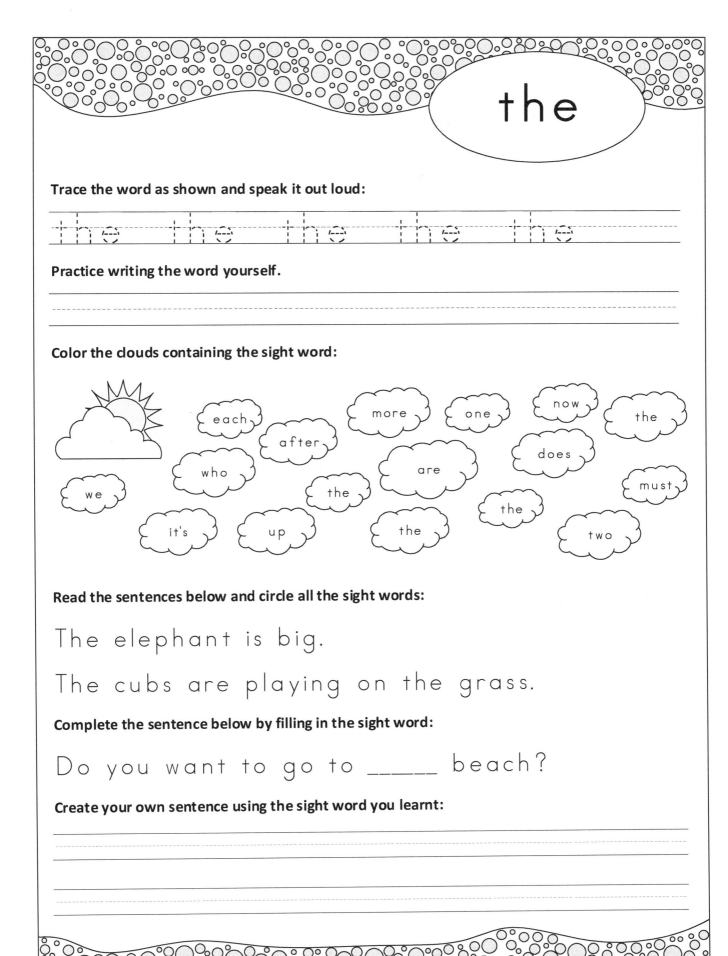

each

after

more   one   now   the

who

does

are

we

must

it's   up   the   the

the

two

Read the sentences below and circle all the sight words:

The elephant is big.

The cubs are playing on the grass.

Complete the sentence below by filling in the sight word:

Do you want to go to _____ beach?

Create your own sentence using the sight word you learnt:

is

Trace the word as shown and speak it out loud:

is   is   is   is   is   is   is   is

Practice writing the word yourself.

Color the clouds containing the sight word:

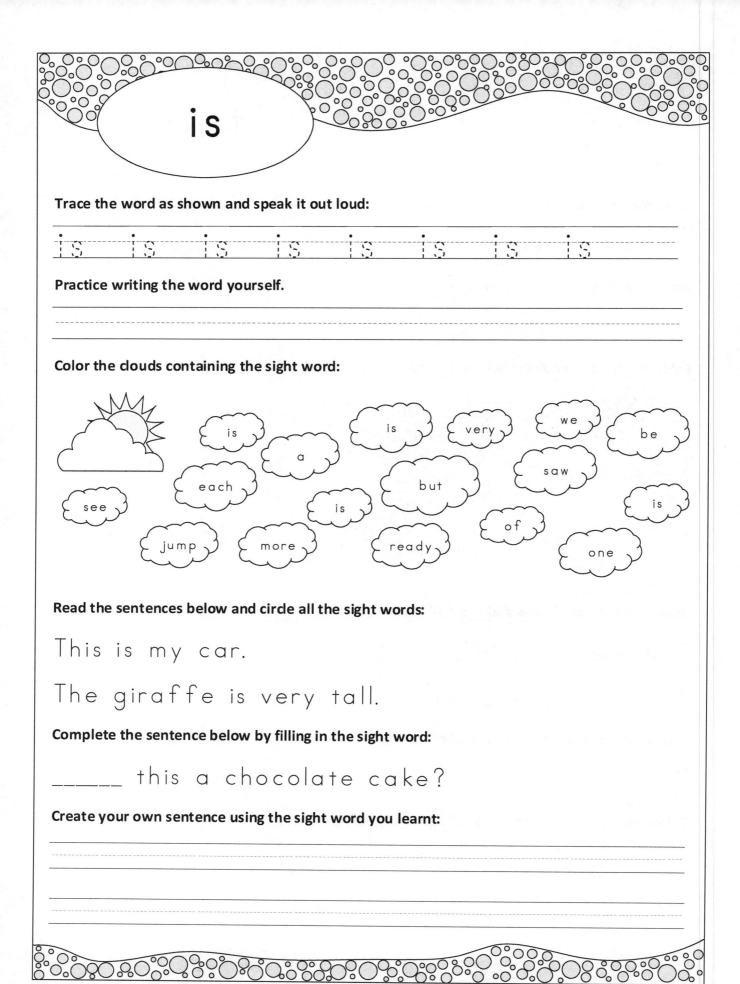

is   very   we   be

a

each   but   saw

see   is   is

jump   more   ready   of

one

Read the sentences below and circle all the sight words:

This is my car.

The giraffe is very tall.

Complete the sentence below by filling in the sight word:

_____ this a chocolate cake?

Create your own sentence using the sight word you learnt:

a

Trace the word as shown and speak it out loud:

a   a   a   a   a   a   a   a

Practice writing the word yourself.

Color the clouds containing the sight word:

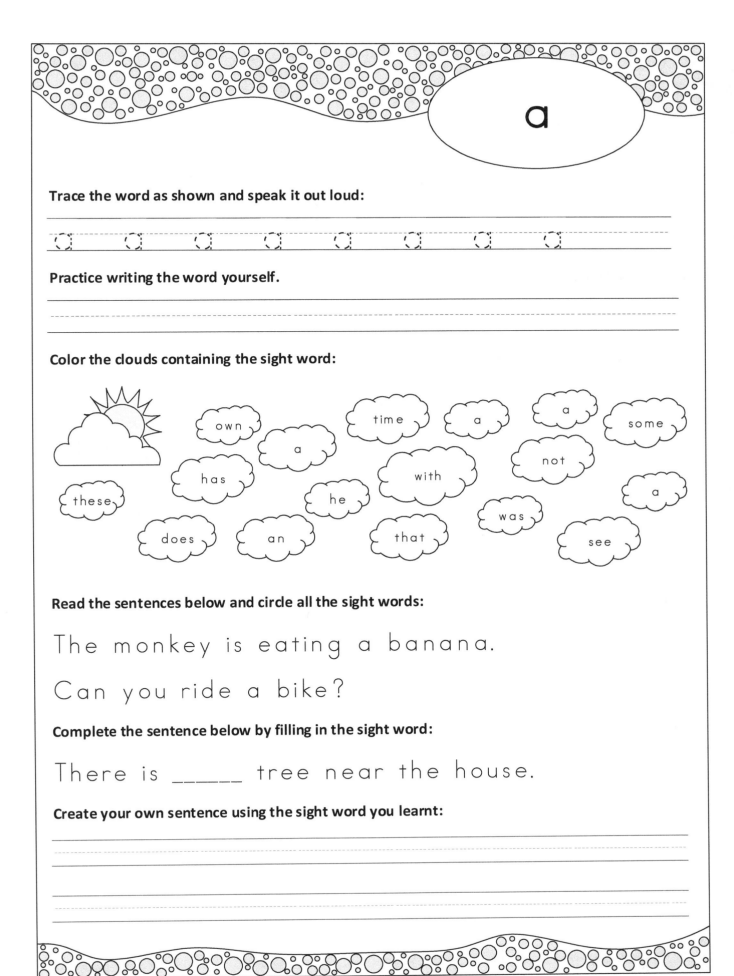

own   time   a   a   some

a   not

has   with

these   he   a

was

does   an   that   see

Read the sentences below and circle all the sight words:

The monkey is eating a banana.

Can you ride a bike?

Complete the sentence below by filling in the sight word:

There is _____ tree near the house.

Create your own sentence using the sight word you learnt:

on

Trace the word as shown and speak it out loud:

on   on   on   on   on   on

Practice writing the word yourself.

Color the clouds containing the sight word:

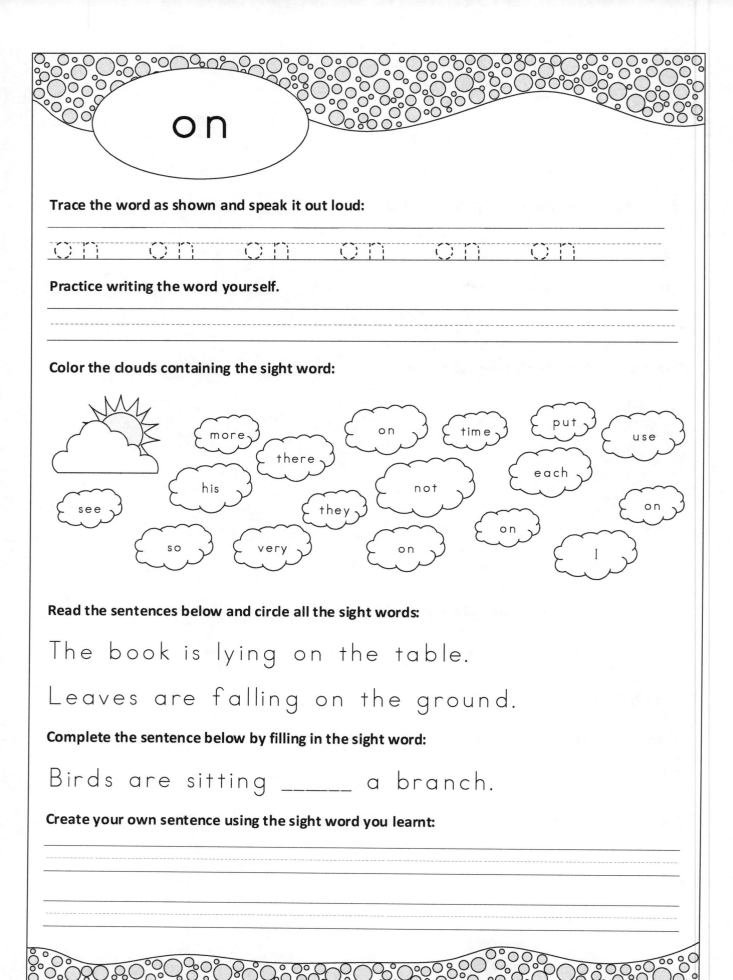

more   there   on   time   put   use

his   not   each

see   they   on

so   very   on   on   I

Read the sentences below and circle all the sight words:

The book is lying on the table.

Leaves are falling on the ground.

Complete the sentence below by filling in the sight word:

Birds are sitting _____ a branch.

Create your own sentence using the sight word you learnt:

I

Trace the word as shown and speak it out loud:

I I I I I I I I I I I

Practice writing the word yourself.

Color the clouds containing the sight word:

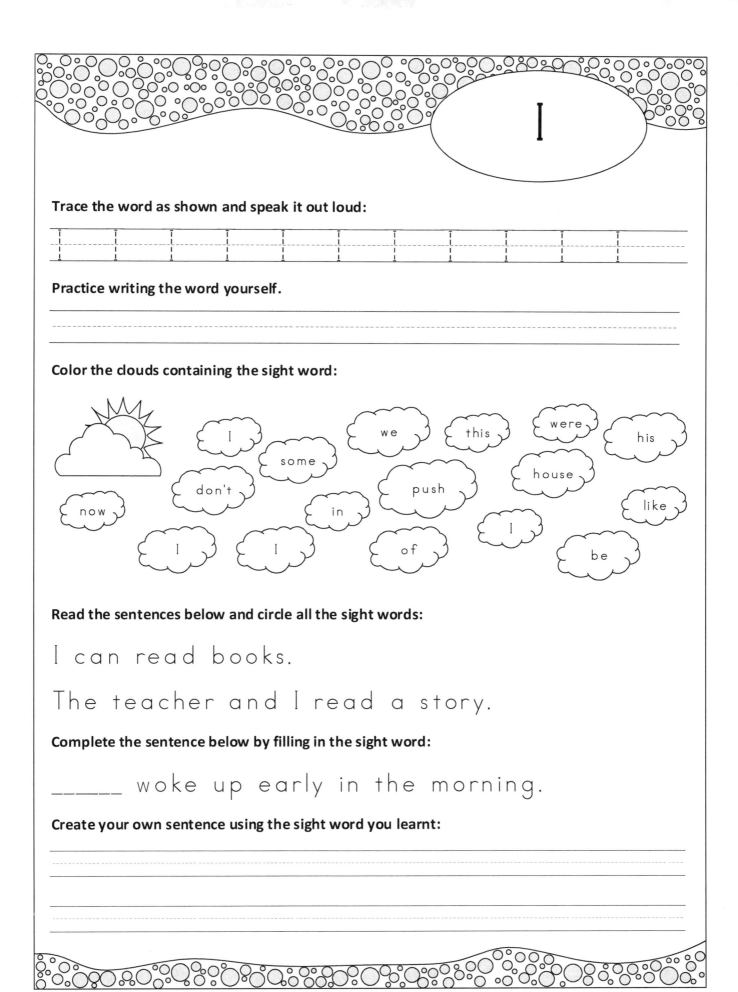

Read the sentences below and circle all the sight words:

I can read books.

The teacher and I read a story.

Complete the sentence below by filling in the sight word:

_____ woke up early in the morning.

Create your own sentence using the sight word you learnt:

it

Trace the word as shown and speak it out loud:

it   it   it   it   it   it   it   it

Practice writing the word yourself.

Color the clouds containing the sight word:

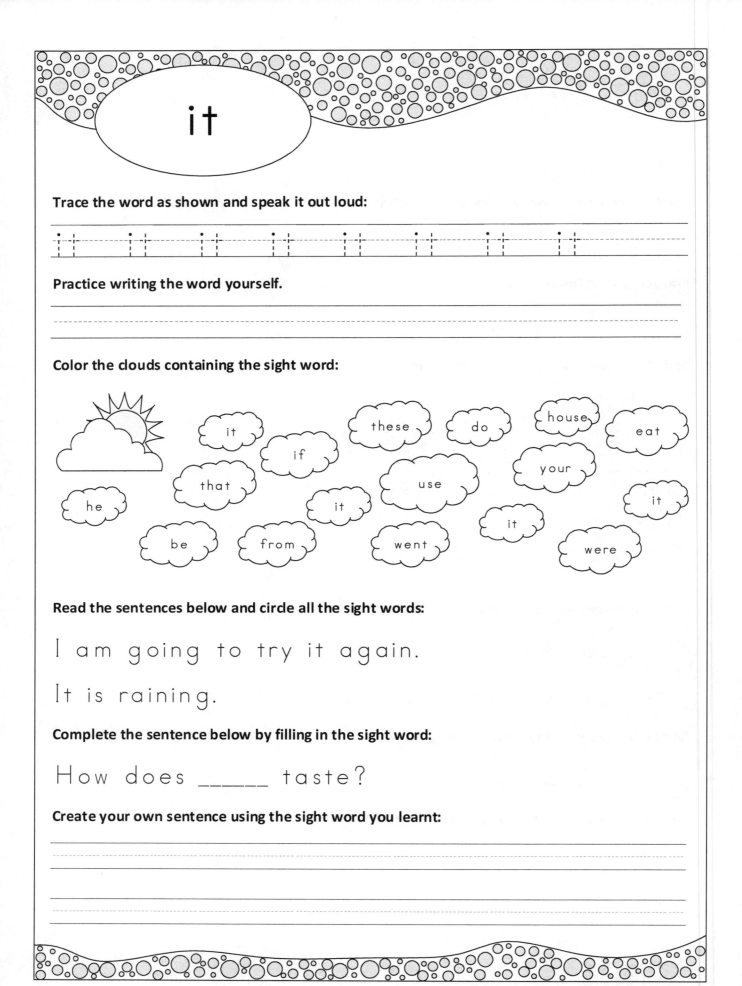

it   if   these   do   house   eat
that   use   your
he   it   it
be   from   went   were

Read the sentences below and circle all the sight words:

I am going to try it again.

It is raining.

Complete the sentence below by filling in the sight word:

How does _____ taste?

Create your own sentence using the sight word you learnt:

too

Trace the word as shown and speak it out loud:

too   too   too   too   too

Practice writing the word yourself.

Color the clouds containing the sight word:

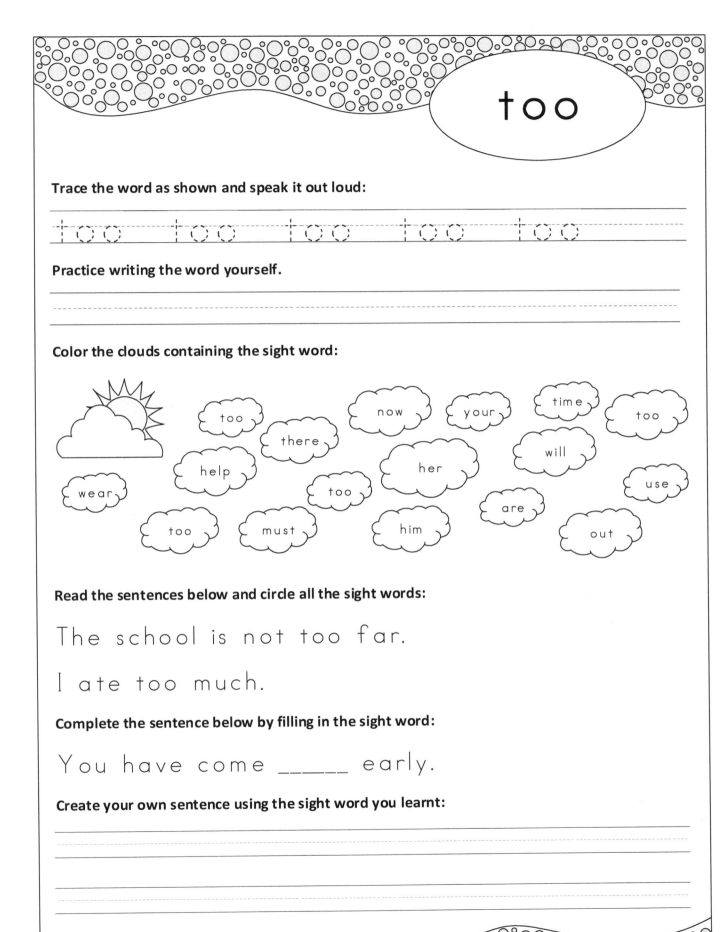

Read the sentences below and circle all the sight words:

The school is not too far.

I ate too much.

Complete the sentence below by filling in the sight word:

You have come _____ early.

Create your own sentence using the sight word you learnt:

for

Trace the word as shown and speak it out loud:

for   for   for   for   for

Practice writing the word yourself.

Color the clouds containing the sight word:

Read the sentences below and circle all the sight words:

The bunny called the deer for help.

The bunny thanked the deer for coming.

Complete the sentence below by filling in the sight word:

The monkey was looking _____ bananas.

Create your own sentence using the sight word you learnt:

and

Trace the word as shown and speak it out loud:

and   and   and   and

Practice writing the word yourself.

Color the clouds containing the sight word:

one   me   went   our   don't
and   eat
own   was   an
ate
and   it   it's   and   use
                and

Read the sentences below and circle all the sight words:

The turtle and the rabbit are friends.

Please and thank you are magic words.

Complete the sentence below by filling in the sight word:

He likes peanut butter _____ jelly.

Create your own sentence using the sight word you learnt:

if

Trace the word as shown and speak it out loud:

if   if   if   if   if   if   if

Practice writing the word yourself.

Color the clouds containing the sight word:

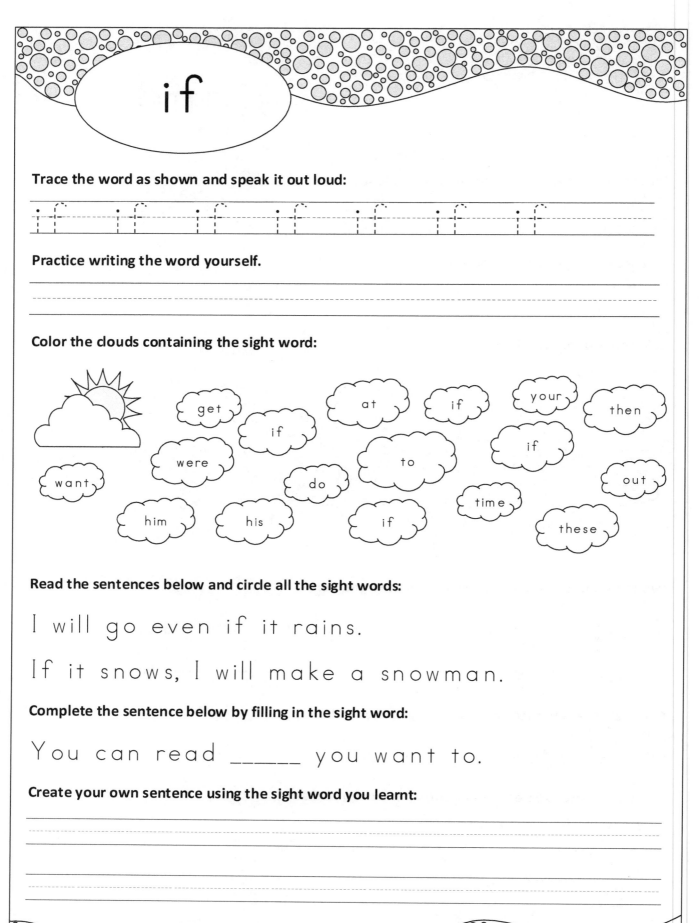

get   at   if   your   then

if   were   to   if   then

want   do   time   out

him   his   if   these

Read the sentences below and circle all the sight words:

I will go even if it rains.

If it snows, I will make a snowman.

Complete the sentence below by filling in the sight word:

You can read _____ you want to.

Create your own sentence using the sight word you learnt:

a m

Trace the word as shown and speak it out loud:

a m   a m   a m   a m   a m

Practice writing the word yourself.

Color the clouds containing the sight word:

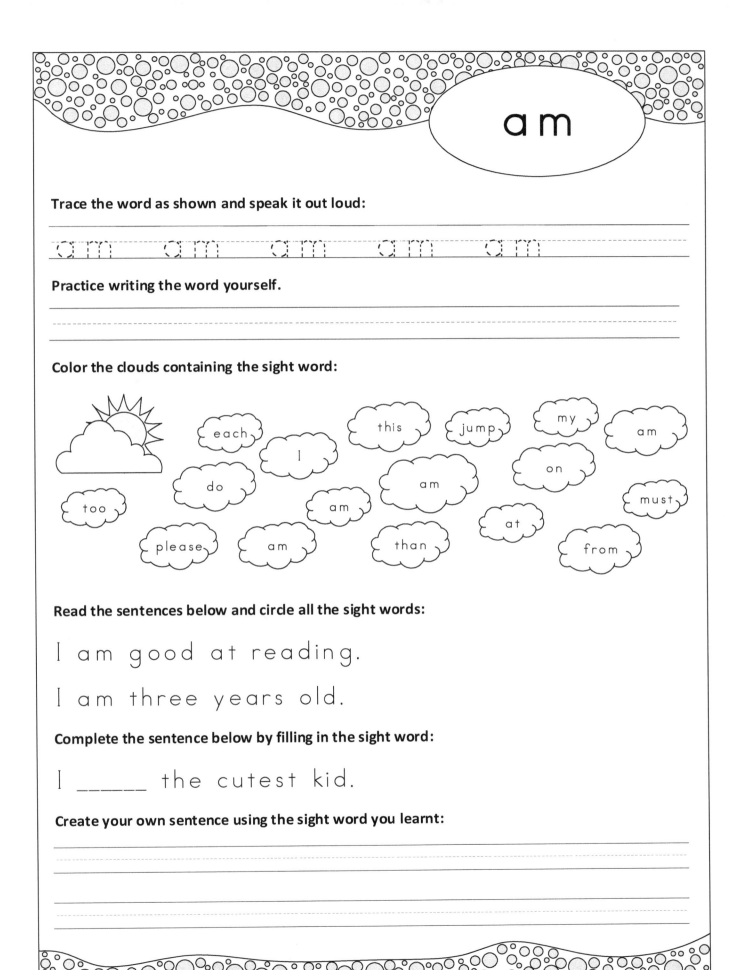

Read the sentences below and circle all the sight words:

I am good at reading.

I am three years old.

Complete the sentence below by filling in the sight word:

I _____ the cutest kid.

Create your own sentence using the sight word you learnt:

or

Trace the word as shown and speak it out loud:

or   or   or   or   or   or   or

Practice writing the word yourself.

Color the clouds containing the sight word:

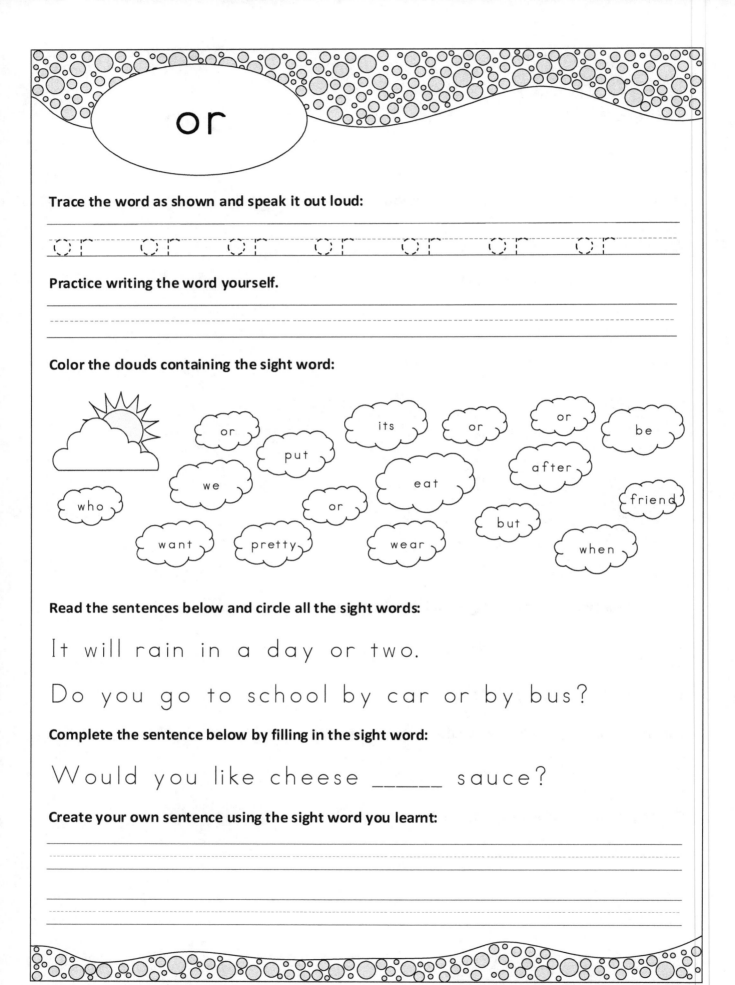

Read the sentences below and circle all the sight words:

It will rain in a day or two.

Do you go to school by car or by bus?

Complete the sentence below by filling in the sight word:

Would you like cheese _____ sauce?

Create your own sentence using the sight word you learnt:

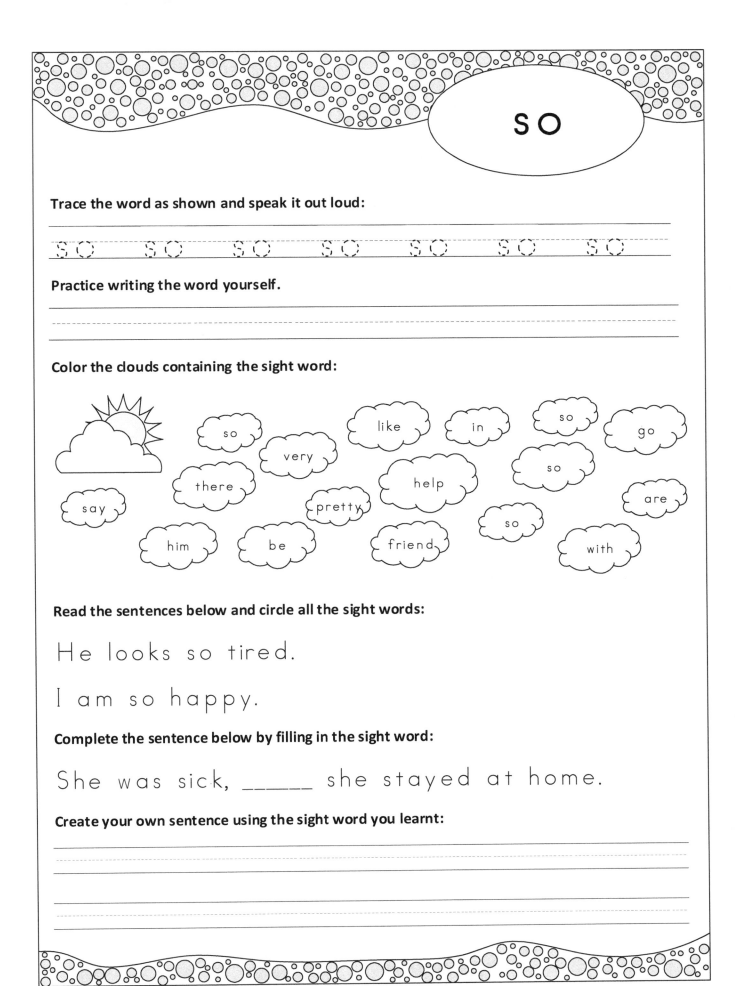

SO

Trace the word as shown and speak it out loud:

SO   SO   SO   SO   SO   SO   SO

Practice writing the word yourself.

Color the clouds containing the sight word:

so   like   in   so   go

very

there   help   so

say   pretty   are

him   be   friend   so   with

Read the sentences below and circle all the sight words:

He looks so tired.

I am so happy.

Complete the sentence below by filling in the sight word:

She was sick, _____ she stayed at home.

Create your own sentence using the sight word you learnt:

go

Trace the word as shown and speak it out loud:

go   go   go   go   go   go

Practice writing the word yourself.

Color the clouds containing the sight word:

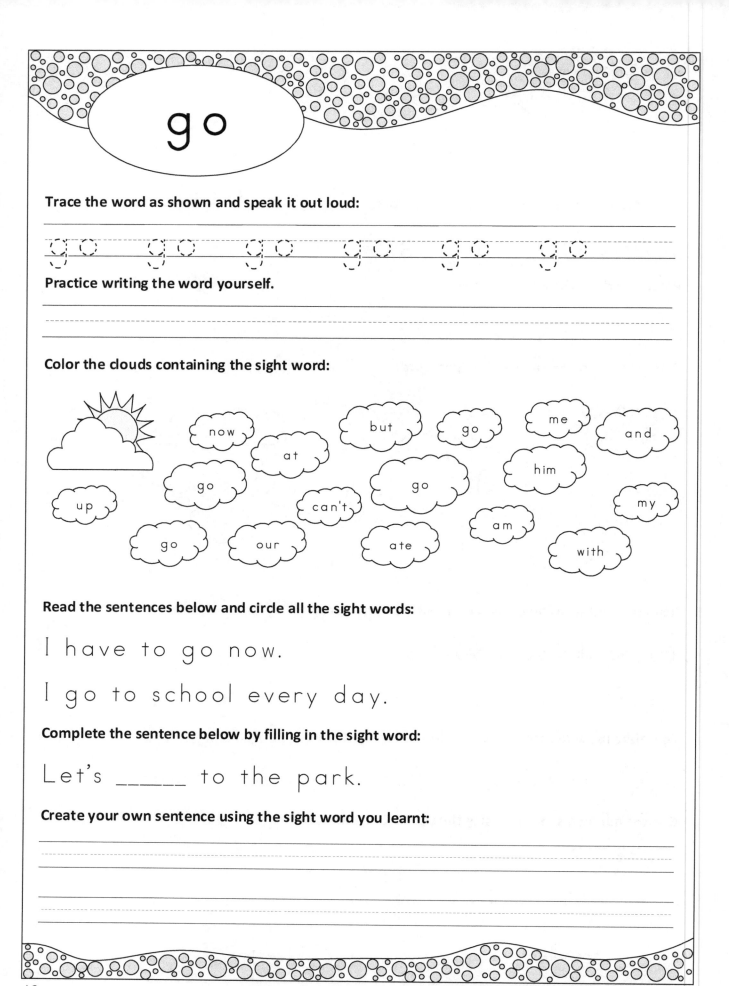

now   at   but   go   me   and

go   go   him

up   can't   my

go   our   ate   am   with

Read the sentences below and circle all the sight words:

I have to go now.

I go to school every day.

Complete the sentence below by filling in the sight word:

Let's _____ to the park.

Create your own sentence using the sight word you learnt:

we

Trace the word as shown and speak it out loud:

we   we   we   we   we   we

Practice writing the word yourself.

Color the clouds containing the sight word:

after   that   her   we   own   than

or   we   am   he

we   we   can't

do   so   get   friend

Read the sentences below and circle all the sight words:

We know how to read.

We are a happy family.

Complete the sentence below by filling in the sight word:

Where should _____ go?

Create your own sentence using the sight word you learnt:

his

Trace the word as shown and speak it out loud:

his   his   his   his   his   his

Practice writing the word yourself.

Color the clouds containing the sight word:

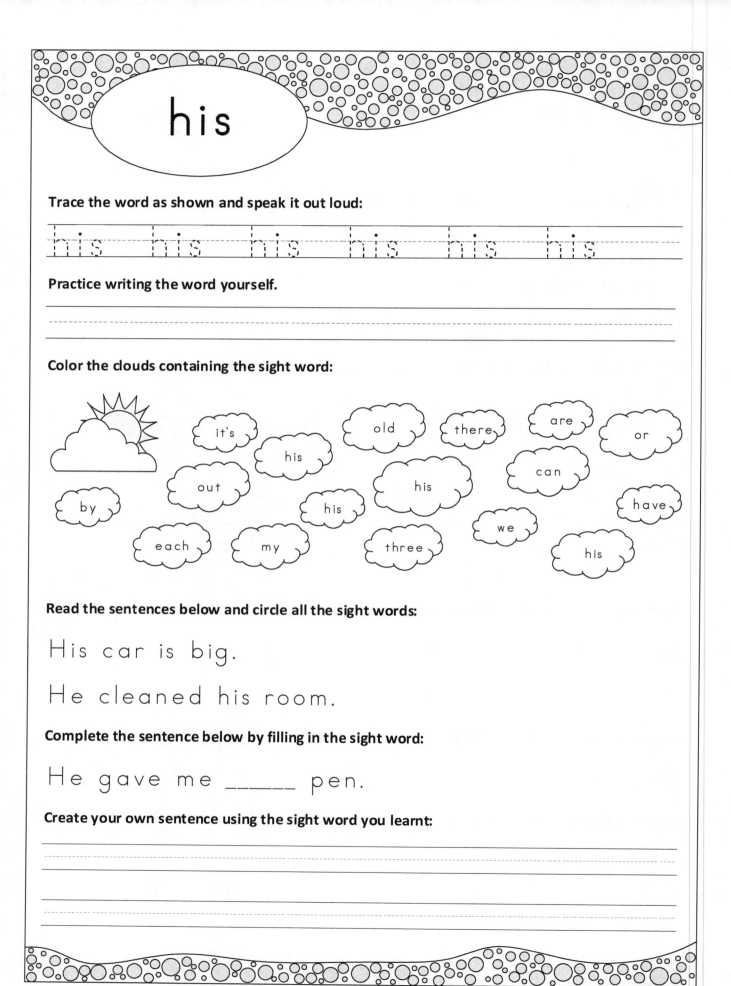

it's   his   old   there   are   or

out   by   his   his   can   have

each   my   three   we   his

Read the sentences below and circle all the sight words:

His car is big.

He cleaned his room.

Complete the sentence below by filling in the sight word:

He gave me _____ pen.

Create your own sentence using the sight word you learnt:

be

Trace the word as shown and speak it out loud:

be   be   be   be   be   be

Practice writing the word yourself.

Color the clouds containing the sight word:

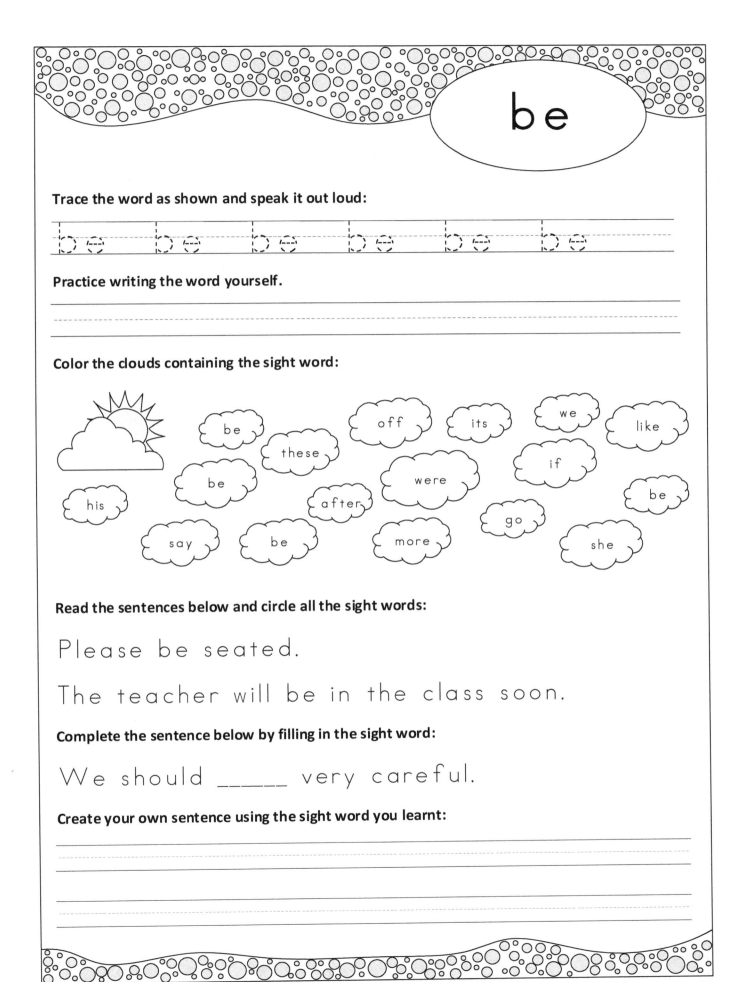

be   these   off   its   we   like

be   his   were   if   be

say   be   after   more   go   she

Read the sentences below and circle all the sight words:

Please be seated.

The teacher will be in the class soon.

Complete the sentence below by filling in the sight word:

We should _____ very careful.

Create your own sentence using the sight word you learnt:

to

Trace the word as shown and speak it out loud:

to   to   to   to   to   to   to

Practice writing the word yourself.

Color the clouds containing the sight word:

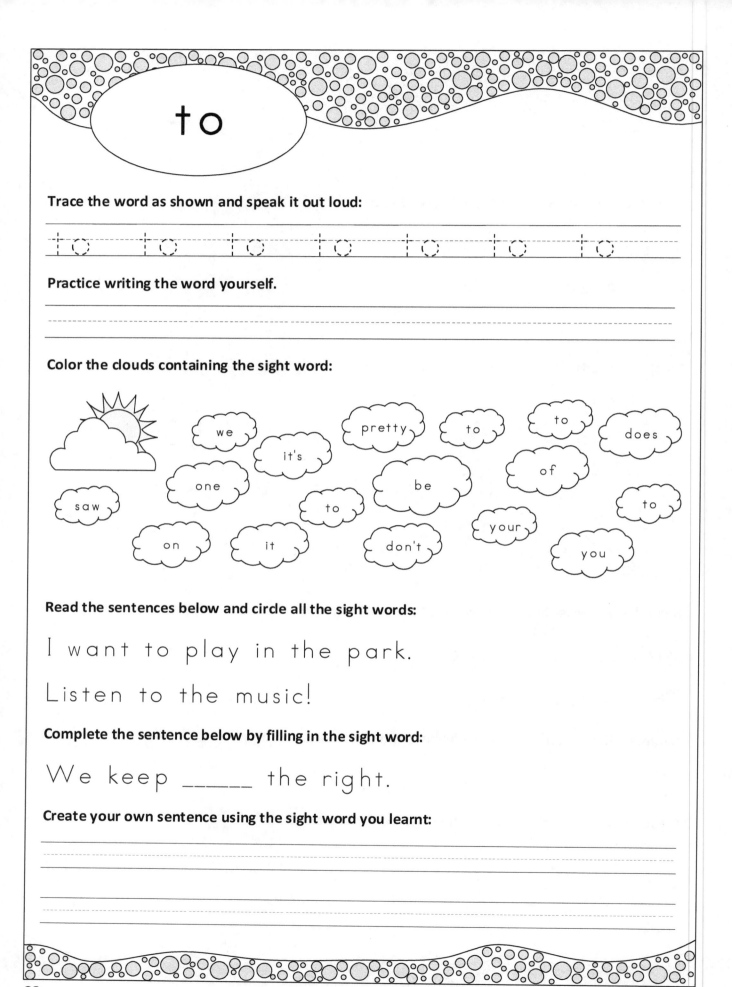

we   it's   pretty   to   to   does

one   be   of

saw   to   your   to

on   it   don't   you

Read the sentences below and circle all the sight words:

I want to play in the park.

Listen to the music!

Complete the sentence below by filling in the sight word:

We keep _____ the right.

Create your own sentence using the sight word you learnt:

who

Trace the word as shown and speak it out loud:

who   who   who   who   who

Practice writing the word yourself.

Color the clouds containing the sight word:

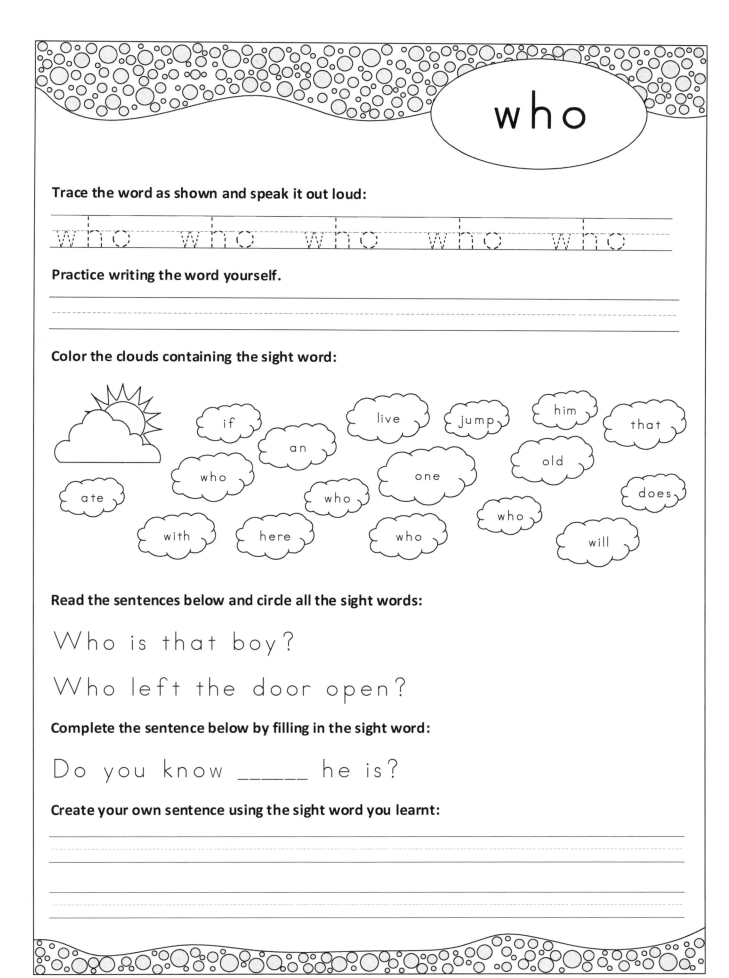

if

an

live   jump   him   that

who

old

ate

one

does

who

with   here   who   who   will

Read the sentences below and circle all the sight words:

Who is that boy?

Who left the door open?

Complete the sentence below by filling in the sight word:

Do you know _____ he is?

Create your own sentence using the sight word you learnt:

off

Trace the word as shown and speak it out loud:

off off off off off

Practice writing the word yourself.

Color the clouds containing the sight word:

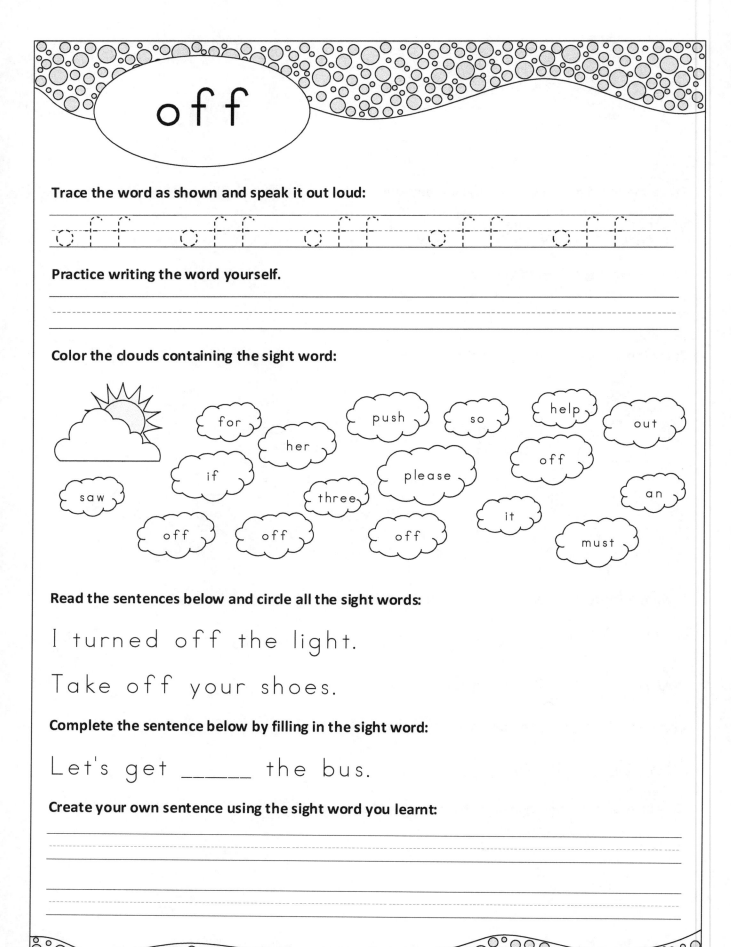

for push so help out

her off

if please an

saw three

off off off it must

Read the sentences below and circle all the sight words:

I turned off the light.

Take off your shoes.

Complete the sentence below by filling in the sight word:

Let's get _____ the bus.

Create your own sentence using the sight word you learnt:

up

Trace the word as shown and speak it out loud:

up   up   up   up   up   up

Practice writing the word yourself.

Color the clouds containing the sight word:

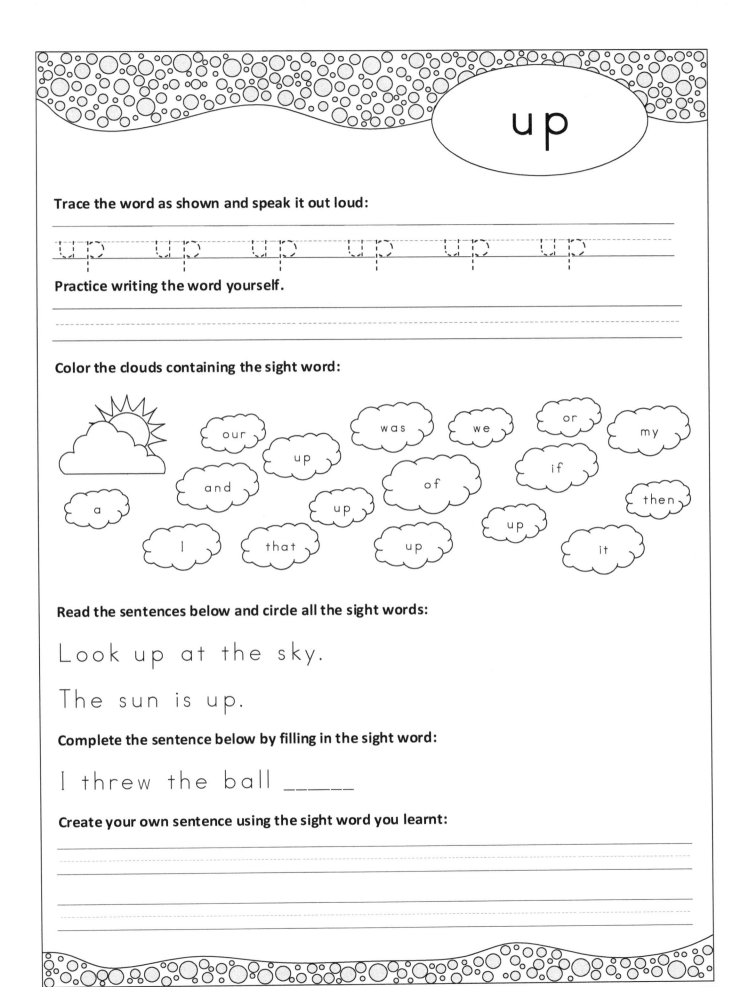

our   was   we   or   my
up
and   of   if
a   up   then
I   that   up   up   it

Read the sentences below and circle all the sight words:

Look up at the sky.

The sun is up.

Complete the sentence below by filling in the sight word:

I threw the ball _____

Create your own sentence using the sight word you learnt:

my

Trace the word as shown and speak it out loud:

my my my my my my

Practice writing the word yourself.

Color the clouds containing the sight word:

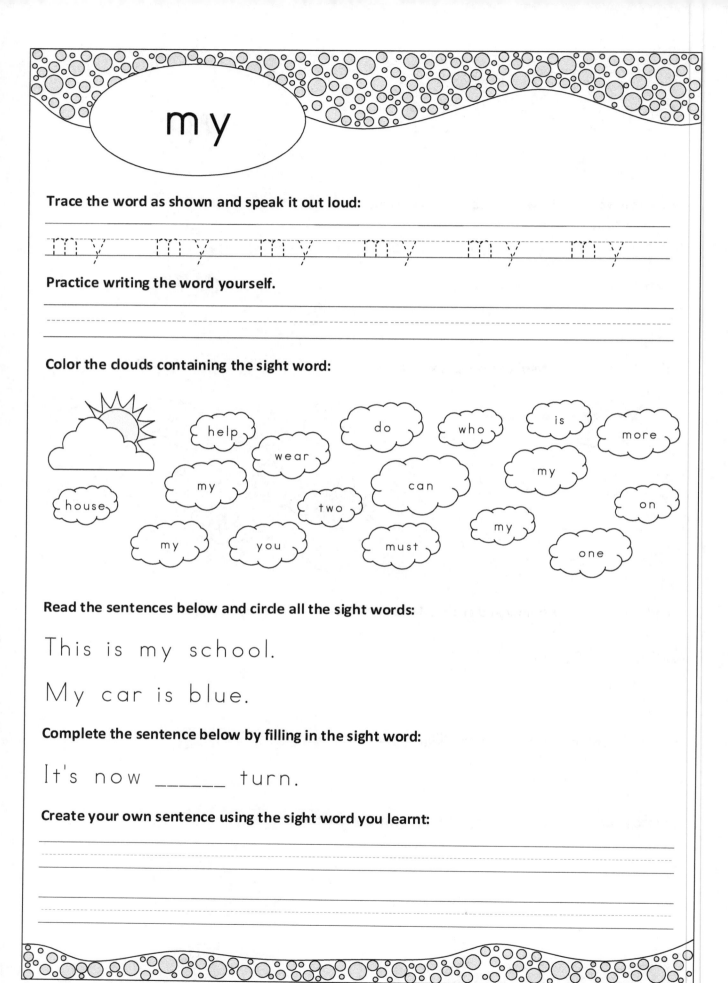

Read the sentences below and circle all the sight words:

This is my school.

My car is blue.

Complete the sentence below by filling in the sight word:

It's now _____ turn.

Create your own sentence using the sight word you learnt:

in

Trace the word as shown and speak it out loud:

in   in   in   in   in   in   in

Practice writing the word yourself.

Color the clouds containing the sight word:

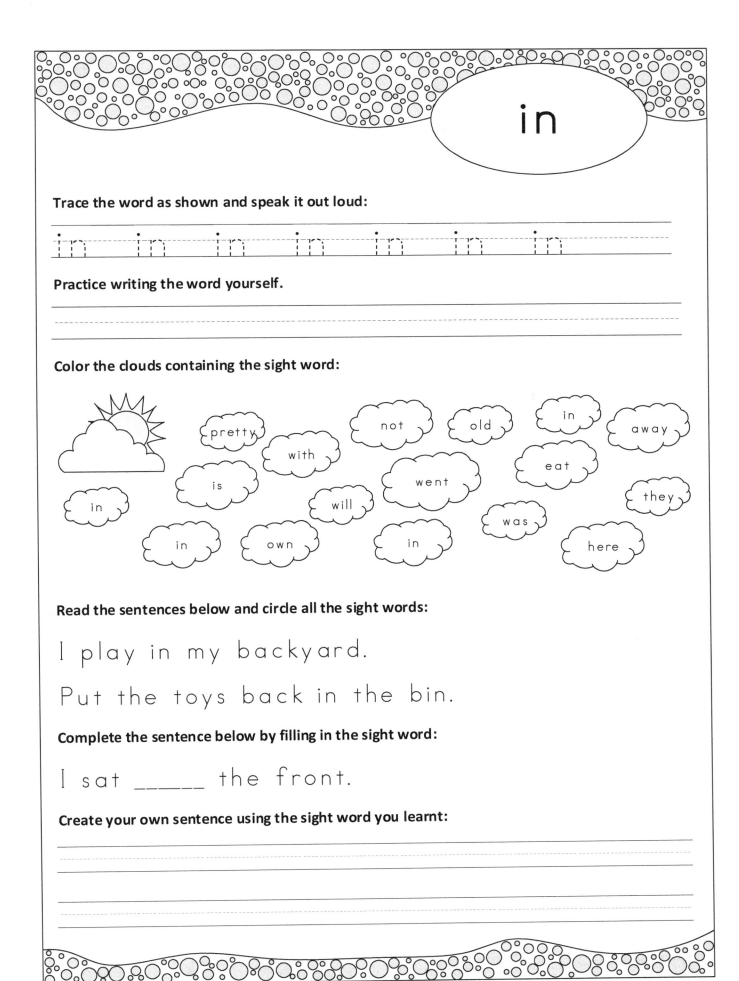

pretty with not old in away
is went eat
in will they
in own in was here

Read the sentences below and circle all the sight words:

I play in my backyard.

Put the toys back in the bin.

Complete the sentence below by filling in the sight word:

I sat _____ the front.

Create your own sentence using the sight word you learnt:

he

Trace the word as shown and speak it out loud:

he   he   he   he   he   he

Practice writing the word yourself.

Color the clouds containing the sight word:

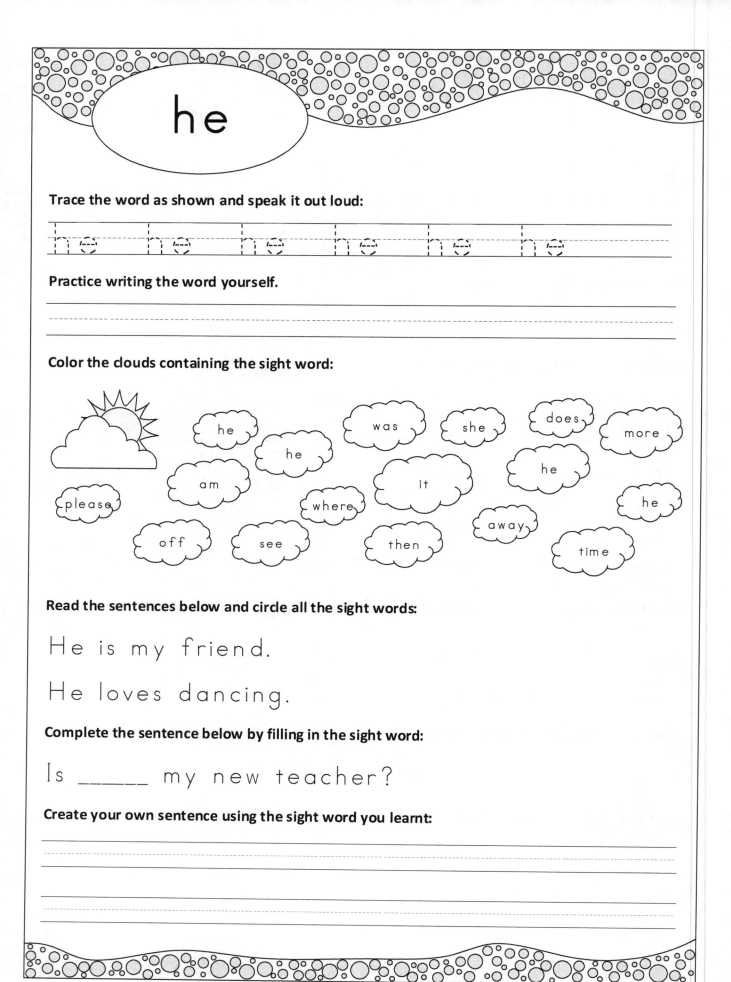

he   he   was   she   does   more

am   it   he

please   where   he

off   see   then   away   time

Read the sentences below and circle all the sight words:

He is my friend.

He loves dancing.

Complete the sentence below by filling in the sight word:

Is _____ my new teacher?

Create your own sentence using the sight word you learnt:

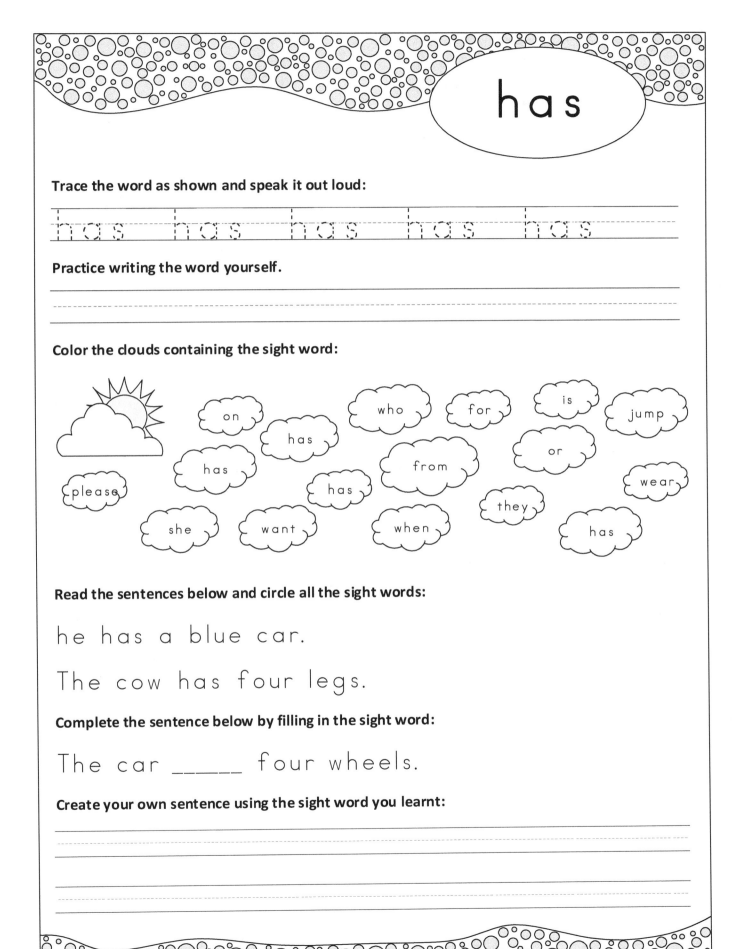

has

Trace the word as shown and speak it out loud:

has   has   has   has   has

Practice writing the word yourself.

Color the clouds containing the sight word:

on

has

has

please

she   want

who   for   is   jump

from   or

has   wear

when   they   has

Read the sentences below and circle all the sight words:

he has a blue car.

The cow has four legs.

Complete the sentence below by filling in the sight word:

The car _____ four wheels.

Create your own sentence using the sight word you learnt:

her

Trace the word as shown and speak it out loud:

her her her her her

Practice writing the word yourself.

Color the clouds containing the sight word:

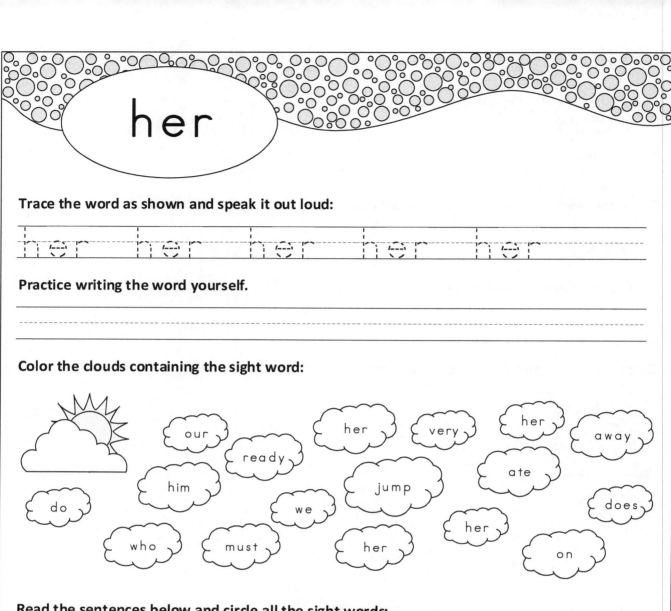

our
her
very
her
away
ready
him
jump
ate
do
we
does
who
must
her
her
on

Read the sentences below and circle all the sight words:

Her eyes are beautiful.

She gave me her book.

Complete the sentence below by filling in the sight word:

She loves _____ cat.

Create your own sentence using the sight word you learnt:

do

Trace the word as shown and speak it out loud:

do   do   do   do   do   do

Practice writing the word yourself.

Color the clouds containing the sight word:

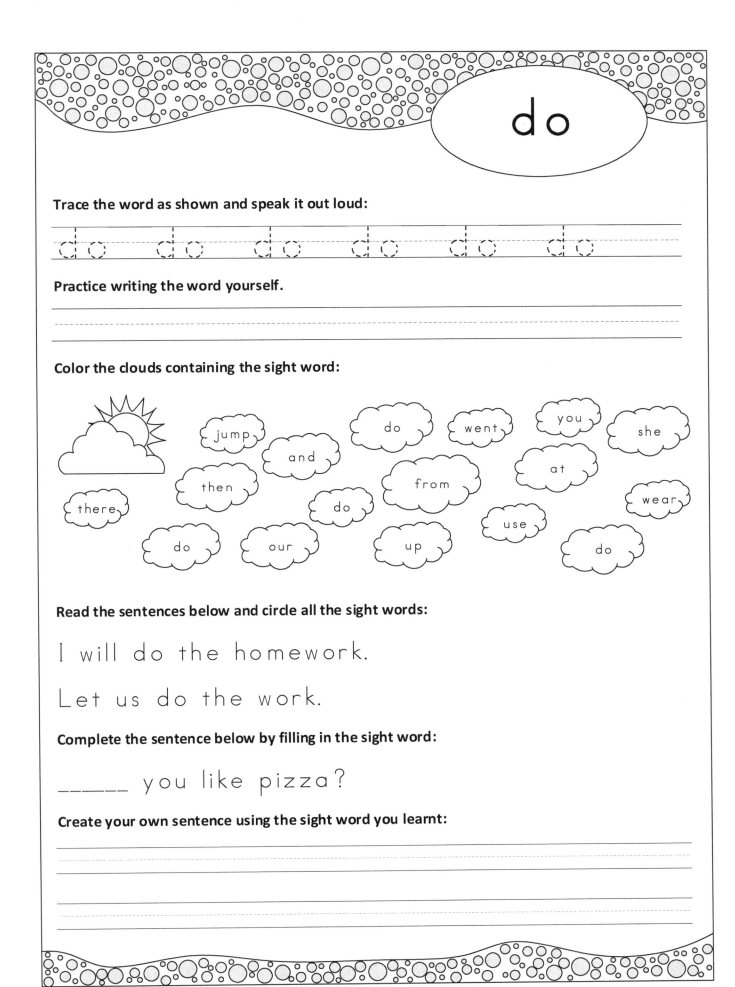

jump   do   went   you   she
and
then   from   at
there   do   wear
do   our   up   use   do

Read the sentences below and circle all the sight words:

I will do the homework.

Let us do the work.

Complete the sentence below by filling in the sight word:

_____ you like pizza?

Create your own sentence using the sight word you learnt:

not

Trace the word as shown and speak it out loud:

not   not   not   not   not

Practice writing the word yourself.

Color the clouds containing the sight word:

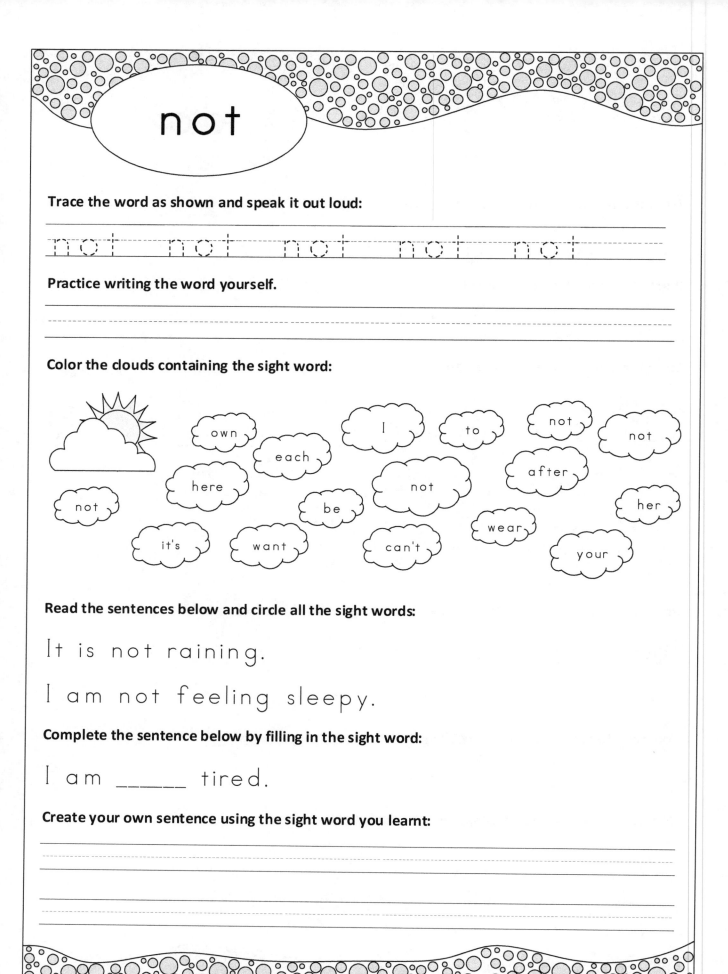

own

each

I

to

not

not

here

not

after

not

be

her

it's

want

can't

wear

your

Read the sentences below and circle all the sight words:

It is not raining.

I am not feeling sleepy.

Complete the sentence below by filling in the sight word:

I am _____ tired.

Create your own sentence using the sight word you learnt:

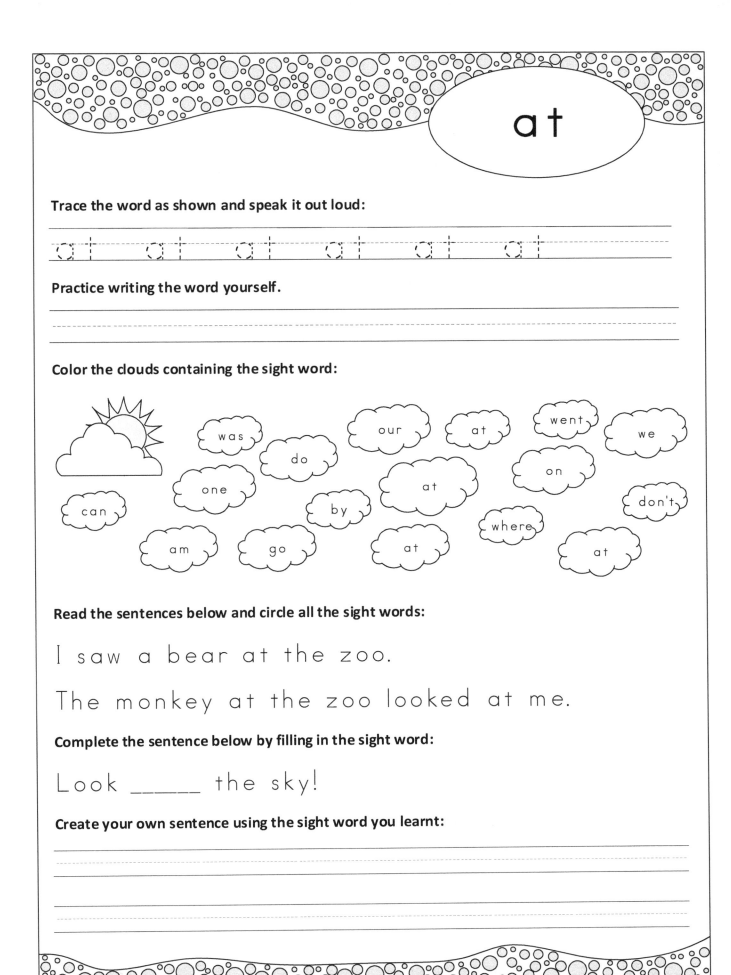

at

Trace the word as shown and speak it out loud:

at   at   at   at   at   at

Practice writing the word yourself.

Color the clouds containing the sight word:

was   our   at   went   we

do

one   at   on

can   by   don't

where

am   go   at   at

Read the sentences below and circle all the sight words:

I saw a bear at the zoo.

The monkey at the zoo looked at me.

Complete the sentence below by filling in the sight word:

Look _____ the sky!

Create your own sentence using the sight word you learnt:

an

Trace the word as shown and speak it out loud:

an   an   an   an   an   an

Practice writing the word yourself.

Color the clouds containing the sight word:

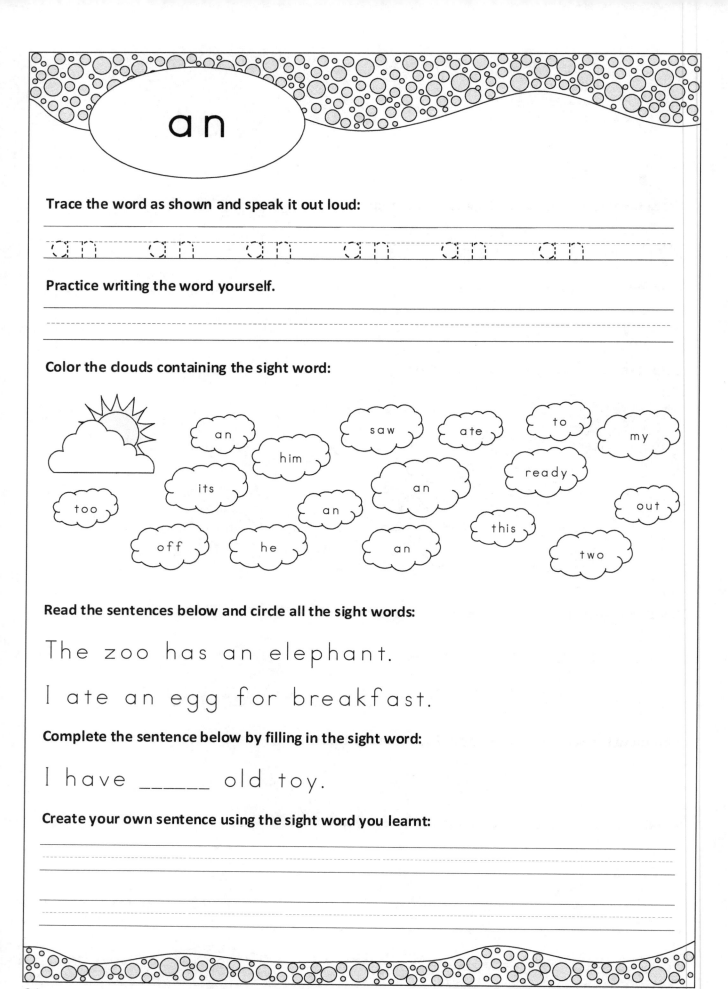

Read the sentences below and circle all the sight words:

The zoo has an elephant.

I ate an egg for breakfast.

Complete the sentence below by filling in the sight word:

I have _____ old toy.

Create your own sentence using the sight word you learnt:

My First Workbook of 100 Sight Words

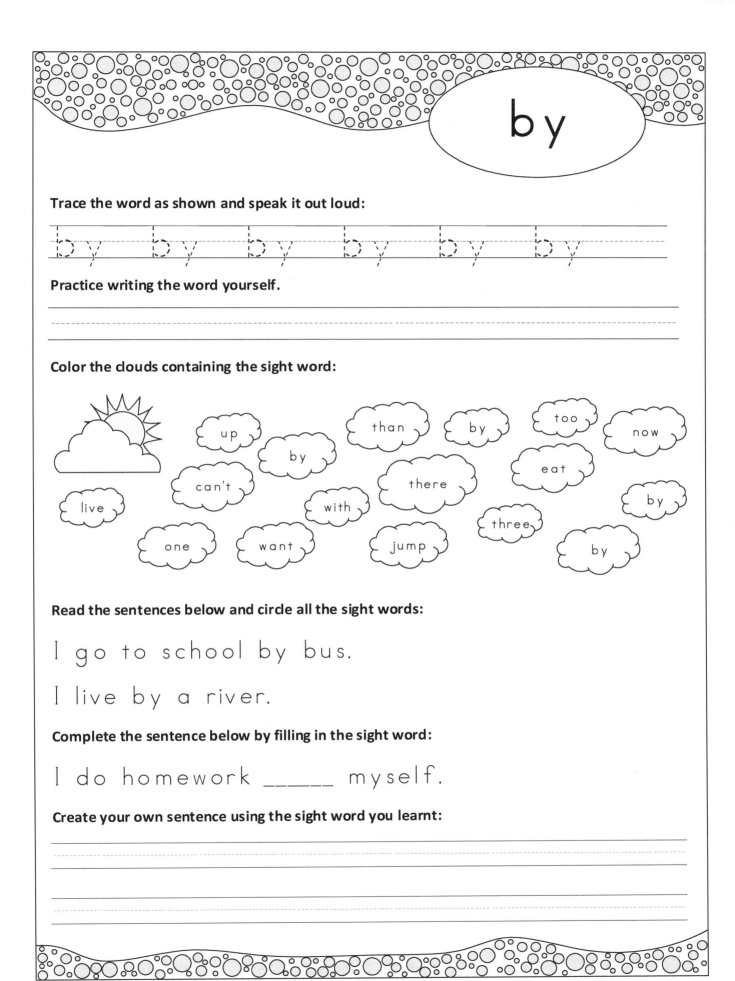

by

Trace the word as shown and speak it out loud:

by   by   by   by   by   by

Practice writing the word yourself.

Color the clouds containing the sight word:

up   than   by   too   now

by   eat

can't   there

live   with   by

three

one   want   jump   by

Read the sentences below and circle all the sight words:

I go to school by bus.

I live by a river.

Complete the sentence below by filling in the sight word:

I do homework _____ myself.

Create your own sentence using the sight word you learnt:

can

Trace the word as shown and speak it out loud:

can   can   can   can   can

Practice writing the word yourself.

Color the clouds containing the sight word:

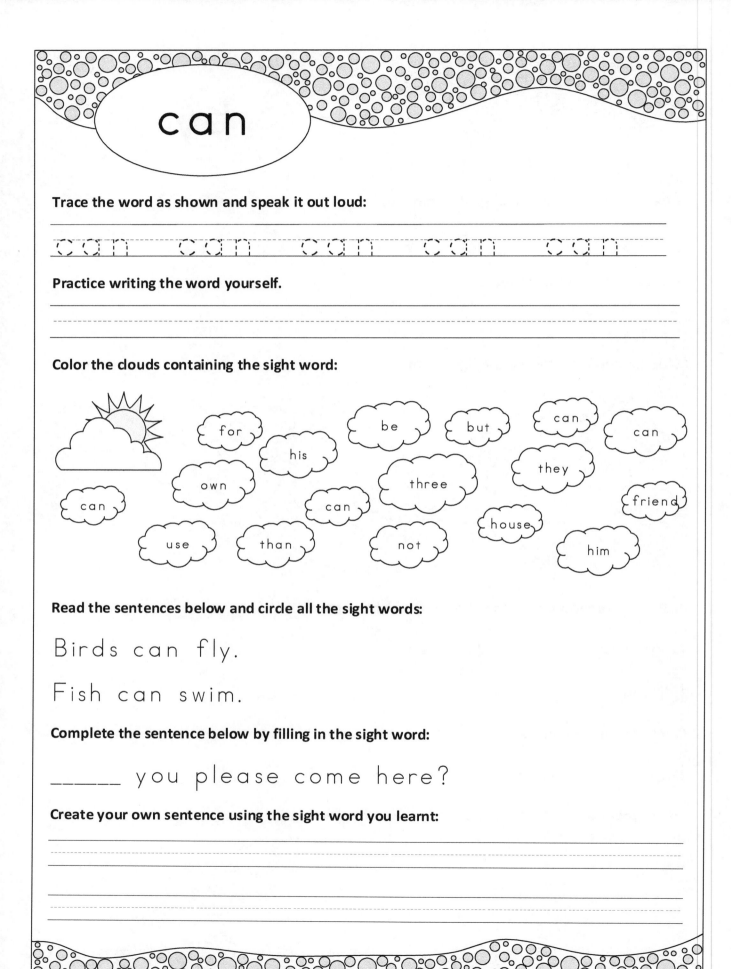

for   be   but   can   can
his
own   three   they
can   friend
use   than   can   house
not   him

Read the sentences below and circle all the sight words:

Birds can fly.

Fish can swim.

Complete the sentence below by filling in the sight word:

_____ you please come here?

Create your own sentence using the sight word you learnt:

you

Trace the word as shown and speak it out loud:

you   you   you   you   you

Practice writing the word yourself.

Color the clouds containing the sight word:

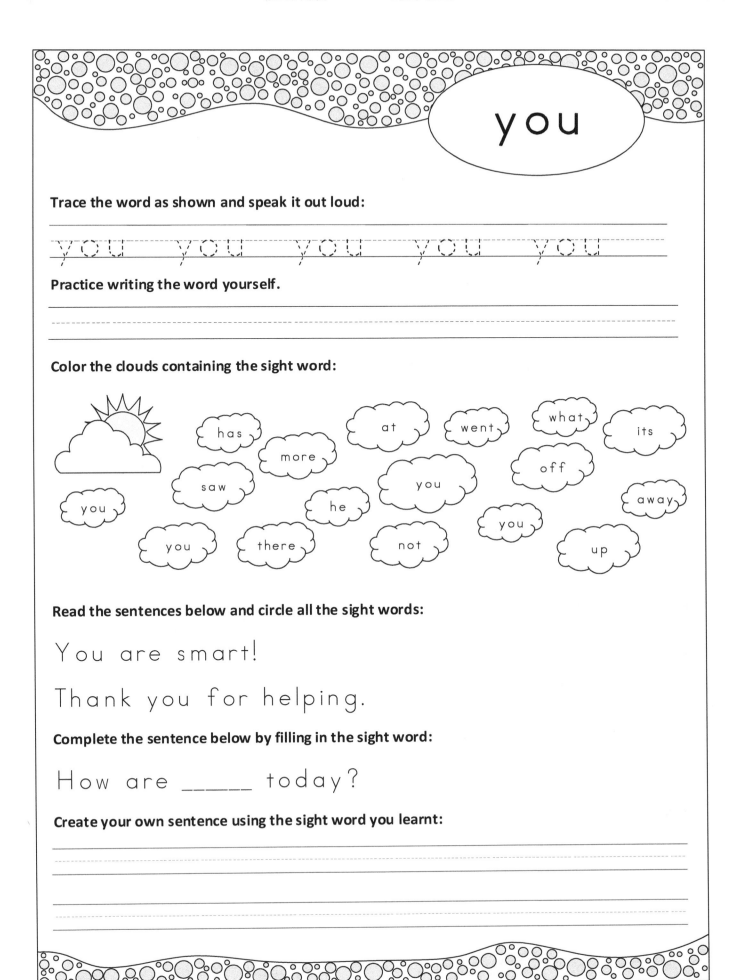

has   more   at   went   what   its

saw   you   off

you   he   you   away

you   there   not   up

Read the sentences below and circle all the sight words:

You are smart!

Thank you for helping.

Complete the sentence below by filling in the sight word:

How are _____ today?

Create your own sentence using the sight word you learnt:

get

Trace the word as shown and speak it out loud:

get   get   get   get   get

Practice writing the word yourself.

Color the clouds containing the sight word:

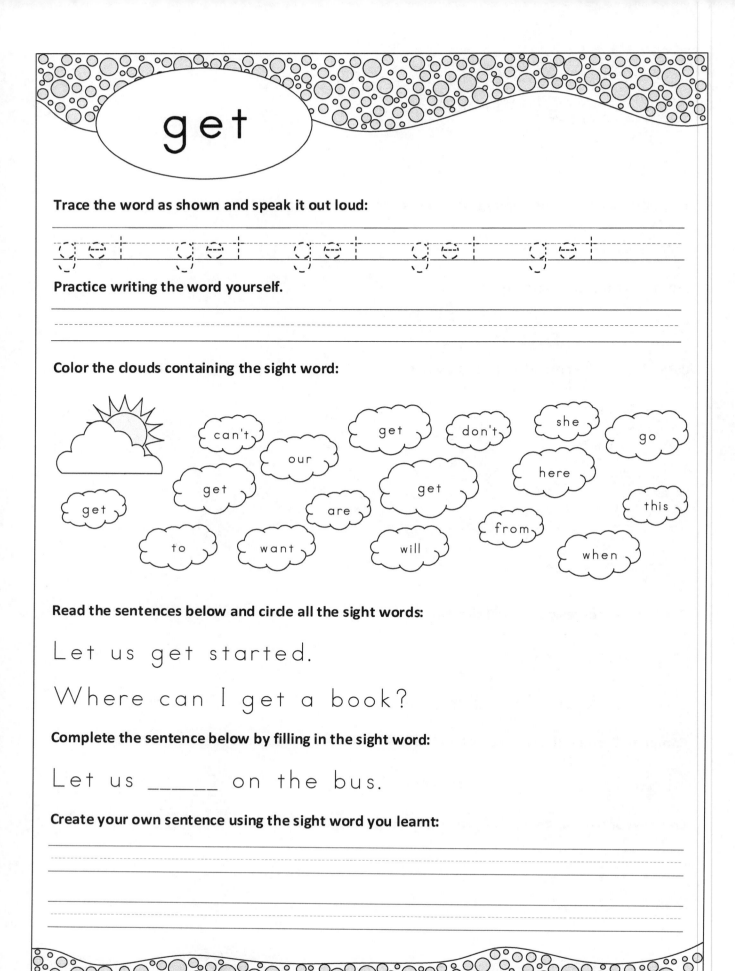

can't

our

get

get

don't

she

go

here

get

get

are

this

to

want

will

from

when

Read the sentences below and circle all the sight words:

Let us get started.

Where can I get a book?

Complete the sentence below by filling in the sight word:

Let us _____ on the bus.

Create your own sentence using the sight word you learnt:

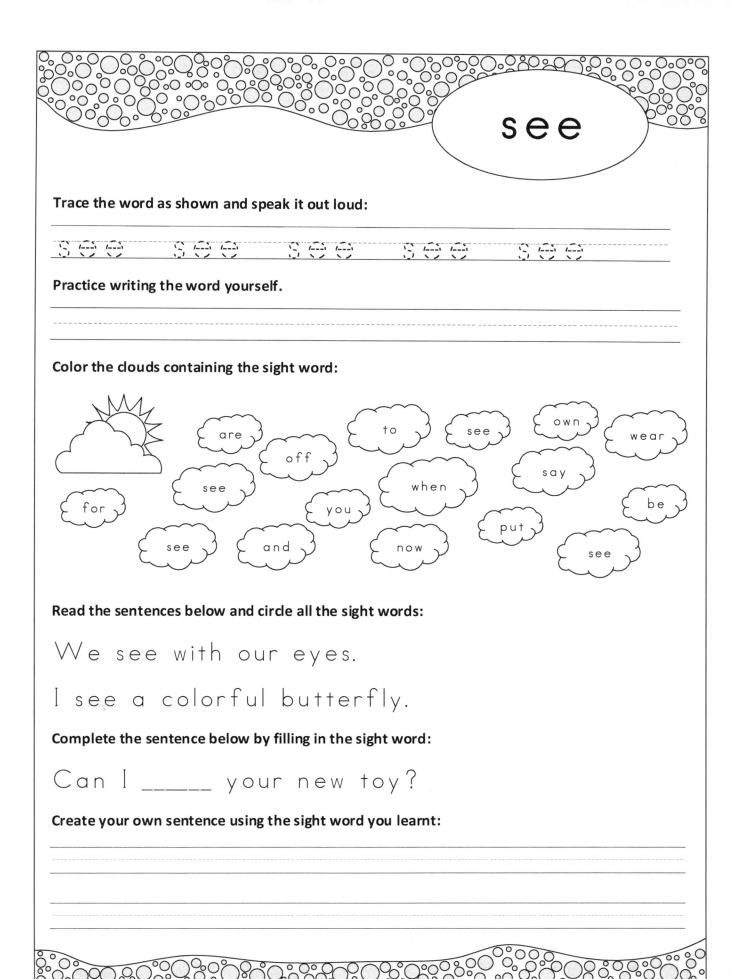

see

Trace the word as shown and speak it out loud:

see   see   see   see   see

Practice writing the word yourself.

Color the clouds containing the sight word:

are   off   to   see   own   wear

see   when   say

for   you   be

see   and   now   put   see

Read the sentences below and circle all the sight words:

We see with our eyes.

I see a colorful butterfly.

Complete the sentence below by filling in the sight word:

Can I _____ your new toy?

Create your own sentence using the sight word you learnt:

of

Trace the word as shown and speak it out loud:

of   of   of   of   of   of   of

Practice writing the word yourself.

Color the clouds containing the sight word:

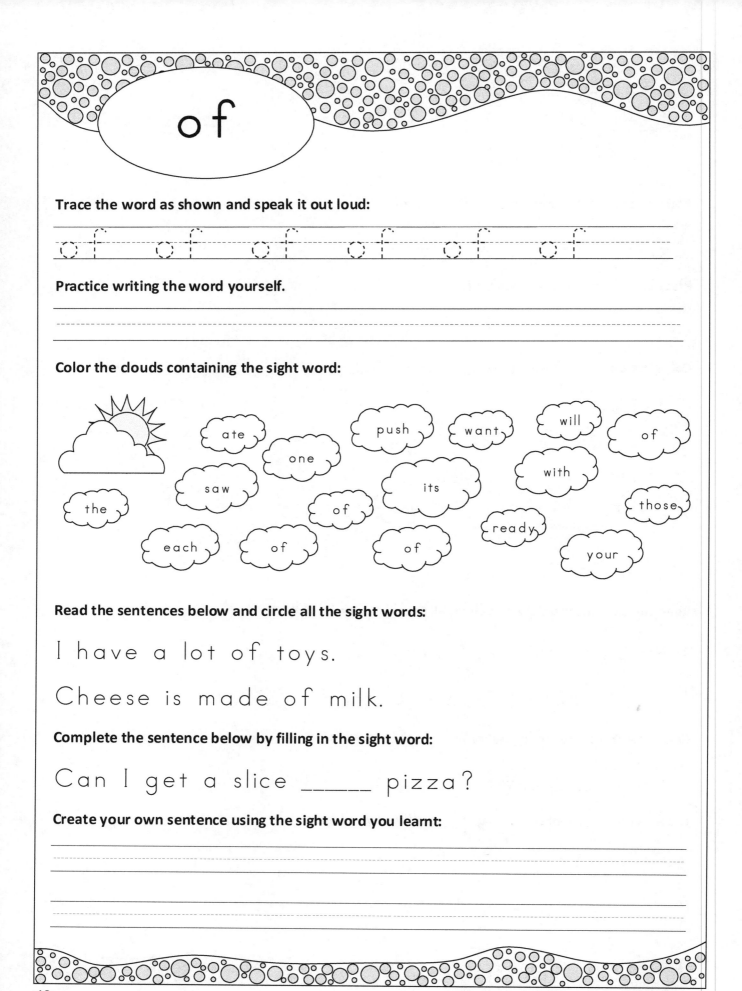

Read the sentences below and circle all the sight words:

I have a lot of toys.

Cheese is made of milk.

Complete the sentence below by filling in the sight word:

Can I get a slice _____ pizza?

Create your own sentence using the sight word you learnt:

will

Trace the word as shown and speak it out loud:

will will will will will

Practice writing the word yourself.

Color the clouds containing the sight word:

some

eat   out   will   off

will

will   am   of

who

in   will

old   I   your   up

friend

Read the sentences below and circle all the sight words:

It will snow today.

I will watch a movie tonight.

Complete the sentence below by filling in the sight word:

_____ it rain tomorrow?

Create your own sentence using the sight word you learnt:

she

Trace the word as shown and speak it out loud:

she   she   she   she   she

Practice writing the word yourself.

Color the clouds containing the sight word:

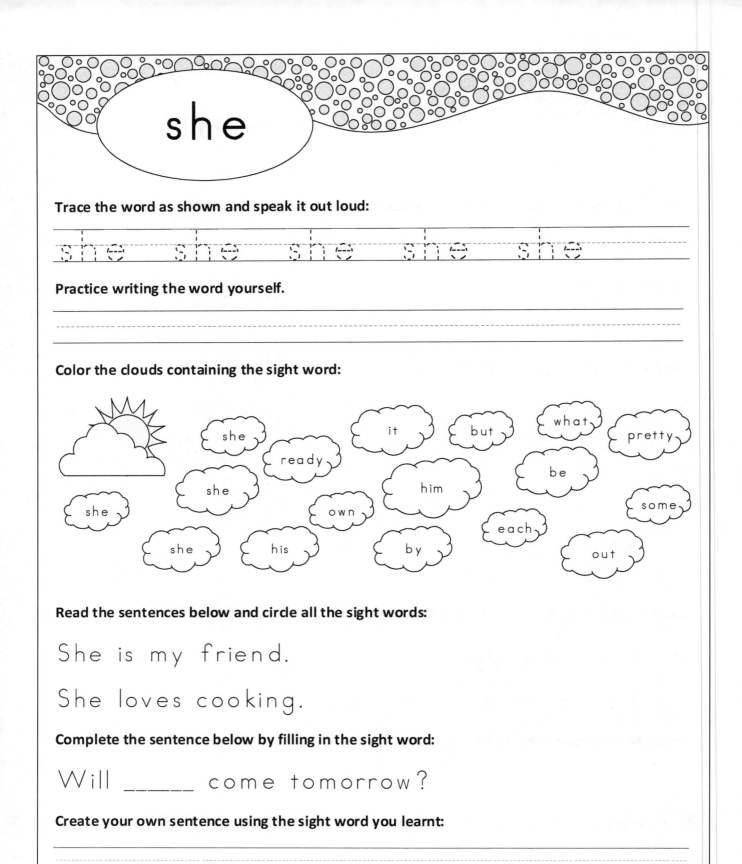

she   ready   it   but   what   pretty
she   be
she   him   some
she   own   each
she   his   by   out

Read the sentences below and circle all the sight words:

She is my friend.

She loves cooking.

Complete the sentence below by filling in the sight word:

Will _____ come tomorrow?

Create your own sentence using the sight word you learnt:

him

Trace the word as shown and speak it out loud:

him   him   him   him   him

Practice writing the word yourself.

Color the clouds containing the sight word:

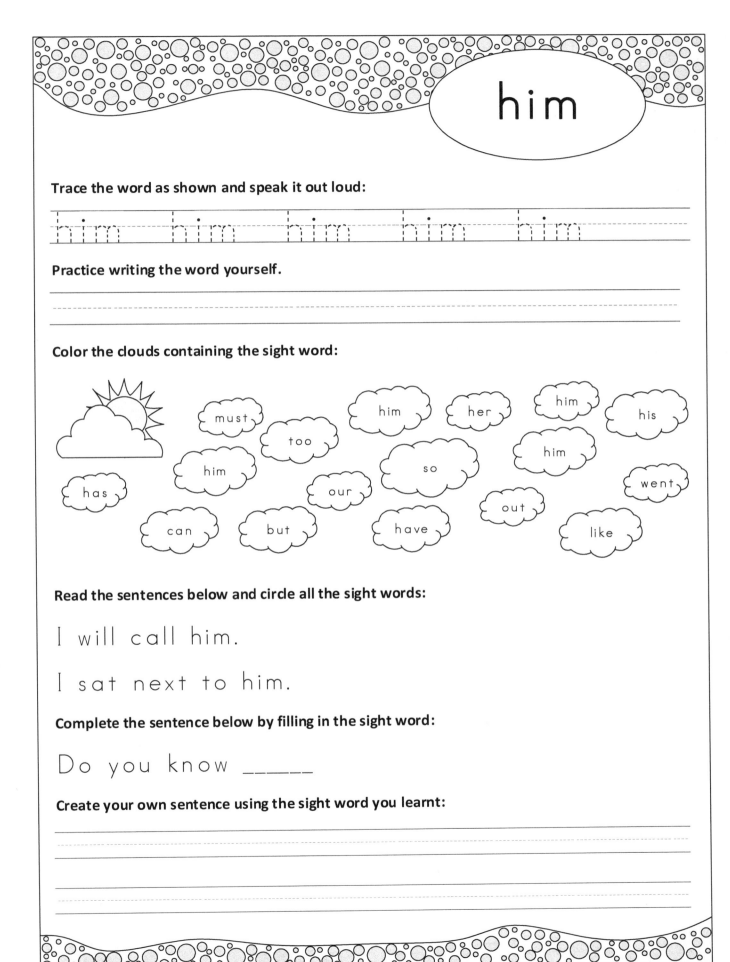

Read the sentences below and circle all the sight words:

I will call him.

I sat next to him.

Complete the sentence below by filling in the sight word:

Do you know _____

Create your own sentence using the sight word you learnt:

are

Trace the word as shown and speak it out loud:

are   are   are   are   are

Practice writing the word yourself.

Color the clouds containing the sight word:

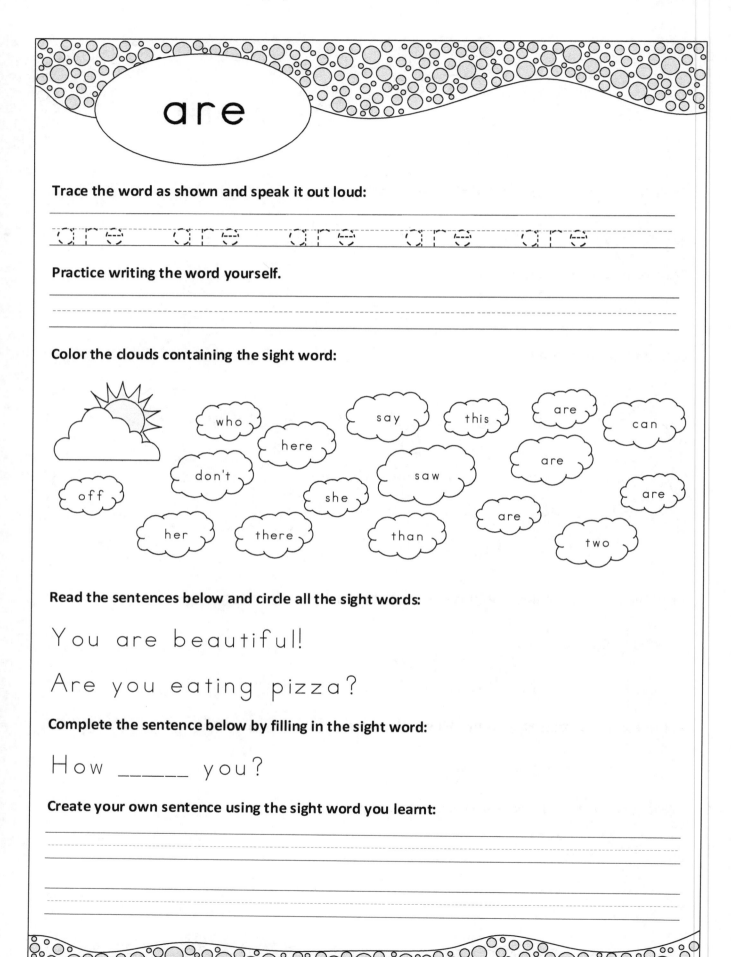

who   here   say   this   are   can

don't   saw   are

off   she   are   are

her   there   than   two

Read the sentences below and circle all the sight words:

You are beautiful!

Are you eating pizza?

Complete the sentence below by filling in the sight word:

How _____ you?

Create your own sentence using the sight word you learnt:

our

Trace the word as shown and speak it out loud:

our   our   our   our   our

Practice writing the word yourself.

Color the clouds containing the sight word:

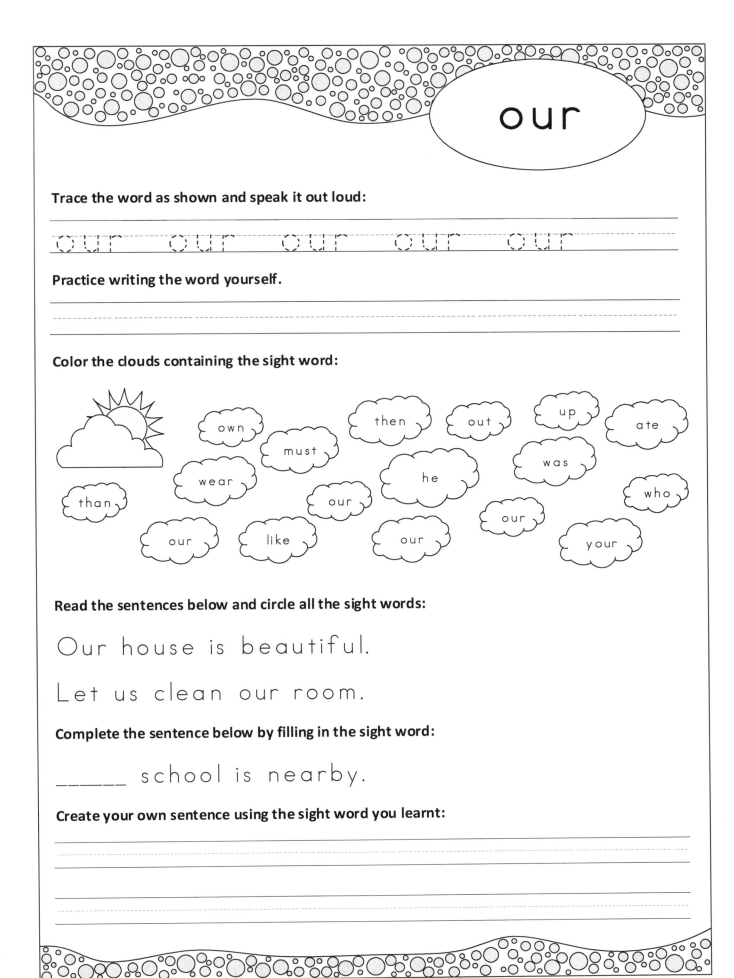

Read the sentences below and circle all the sight words:

Our house is beautiful.

Let us clean our room.

Complete the sentence below by filling in the sight word:

_____ school is nearby.

Create your own sentence using the sight word you learnt:

me

Trace the word as shown and speak it out loud:

me   me   me   me   me

Practice writing the word yourself.

Color the clouds containing the sight word:

Read the sentences below and circle all the sight words:

Gifts make me happy.

My teacher loves me.

Complete the sentence below by filling in the sight word:

Can you help _____

Create your own sentence using the sight word you learnt:

old

Trace the word as shown and speak it out loud:

old   old   old   old   old

Practice writing the word yourself.

Color the clouds containing the sight word:

an

old

if   old   there   to

our   old   time   one   then

old   who   jump   each   after   ate

Read the sentences below and circle all the sight words:

This book is old.

I love our old car.

Complete the sentence below by filling in the sight word:

My friend is four years _____

Create your own sentence using the sight word you learnt:

its

Trace the word as shown and speak it out loud:

its   its   its   its   its   its

Practice writing the word yourself.

Color the clouds containing the sight word:

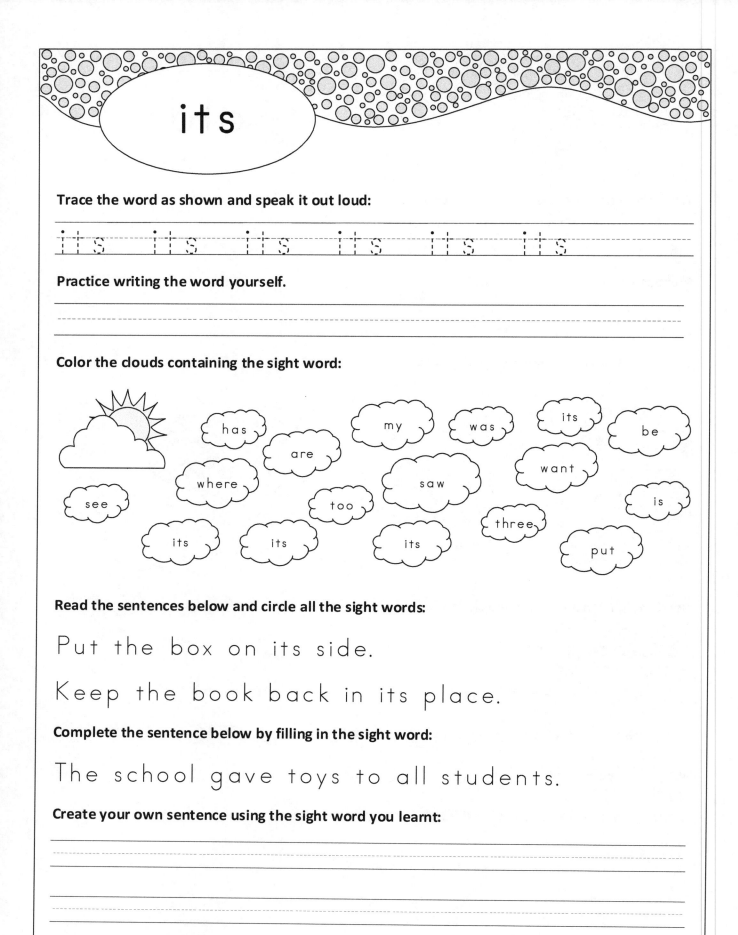

Read the sentences below and circle all the sight words:

Put the box on its side.

Keep the book back in its place.

Complete the sentence below by filling in the sight word:

The school gave toys to all students.

Create your own sentence using the sight word you learnt:

your

Trace the word as shown and speak it out loud:

your   your   your   your

Practice writing the word yourself.

Color the clouds containing the sight word:

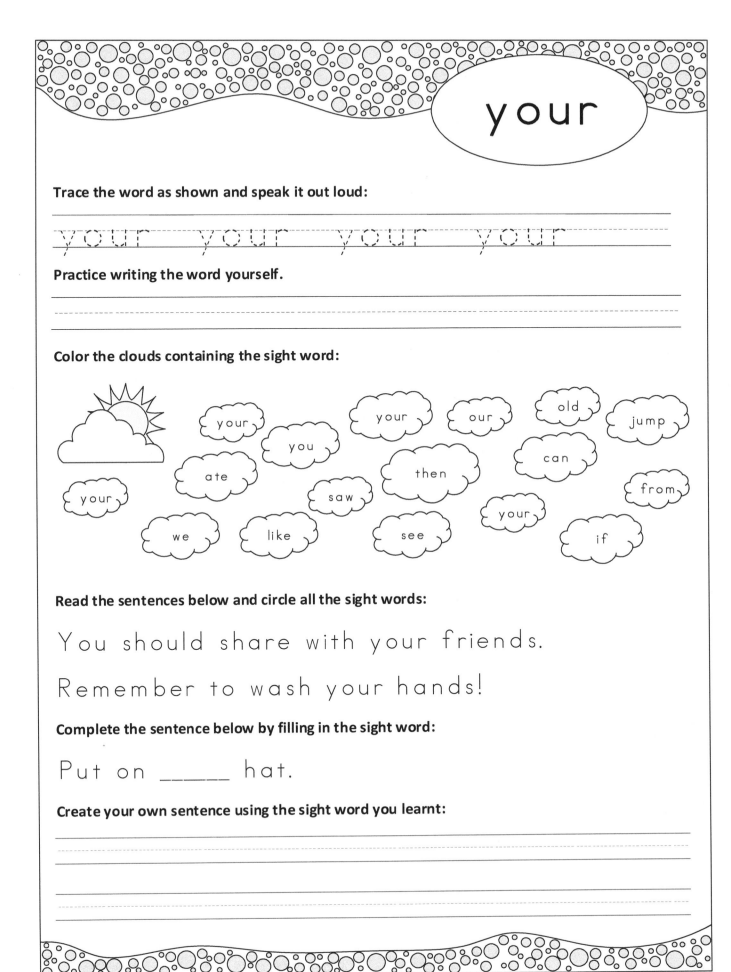

Read the sentences below and circle all the sight words:

You should share with your friends.

Remember to wash your hands!

Complete the sentence below by filling in the sight word:

Put on _____ hat.

Create your own sentence using the sight word you learnt:

but

Trace the word as shown and speak it out loud:

but   but   but   but   but

Practice writing the word yourself.

Color the clouds containing the sight word:

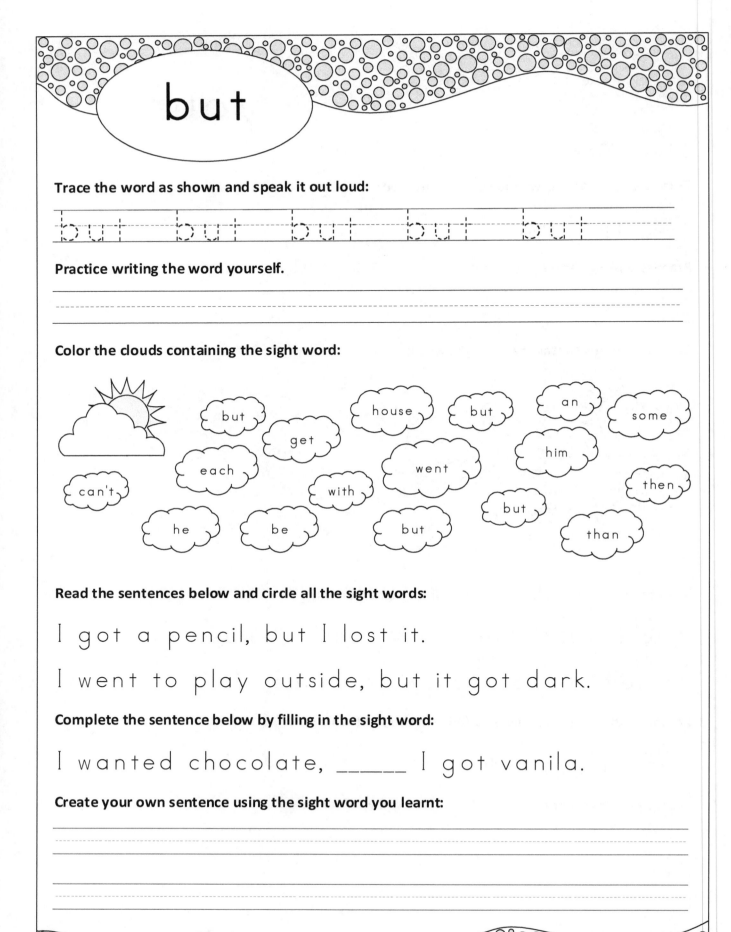

but   house   but   an   some

get   him

each   went   then

can't   with

he   be   but   but

than

Read the sentences below and circle all the sight words:

I got a pencil, but I lost it.

I went to play outside, but it got dark.

Complete the sentence below by filling in the sight word:

I wanted chocolate, _____ I got vanila.

Create your own sentence using the sight word you learnt:

push

Trace the word as shown and speak it out loud:

push   push   push   push

Practice writing the word yourself.

Color the clouds containing the sight word:

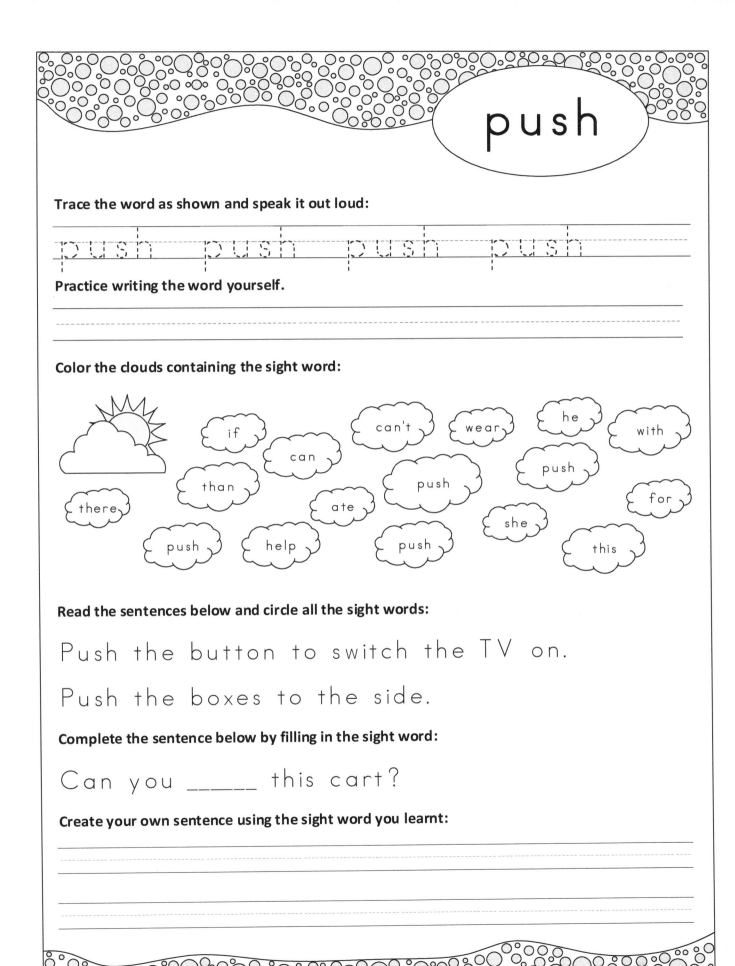

if   can't   wear   he   with
can
than   push   push
there   ate   for
push   help   push   she
this

Read the sentences below and circle all the sight words:

Push the button to switch the TV on.

Push the boxes to the side.

Complete the sentence below by filling in the sight word:

Can you _____ this cart?

Create your own sentence using the sight word you learnt:

help

Trace the word as shown and speak it out loud:

help   help   help   help

Practice writing the word yourself.

Color the clouds containing the sight word:

Read the sentences below and circle all the sight words:

I need help with homework.

She called for help.

Complete the sentence below by filling in the sight word:

May I _____ you?

Create your own sentence using the sight word you learnt:

when

Trace the word as shown and speak it out loud:

when   when   when   when

Practice writing the word yourself.

Color the clouds containing the sight word:

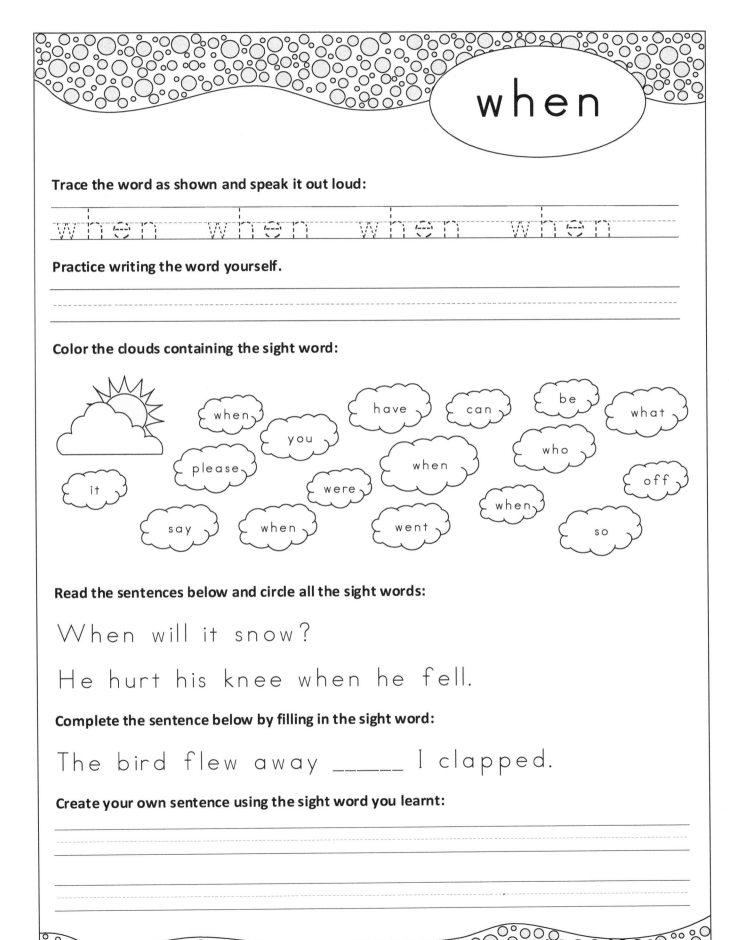

Read the sentences below and circle all the sight words:

When will it snow?

He hurt his knee when he fell.

Complete the sentence below by filling in the sight word:

The bird flew away _____ I clapped.

Create your own sentence using the sight word you learnt:

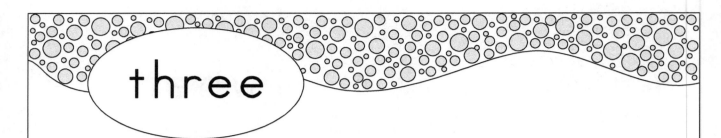

three

Trace the word as shown and speak it out loud:

three   three   three

Practice writing the word yourself.

Color the clouds containing the sight word:

Read the sentences below and circle all the sight words:

I am three years old.

There were three cows in the field.

Complete the sentence below by filling in the sight word:

My tricycle has _____ wheels.

Create your own sentence using the sight word you learnt:

54

went

Trace the word as shown and speak it out loud:

went   went   went   went

Practice writing the word yourself.

Color the clouds containing the sight word:

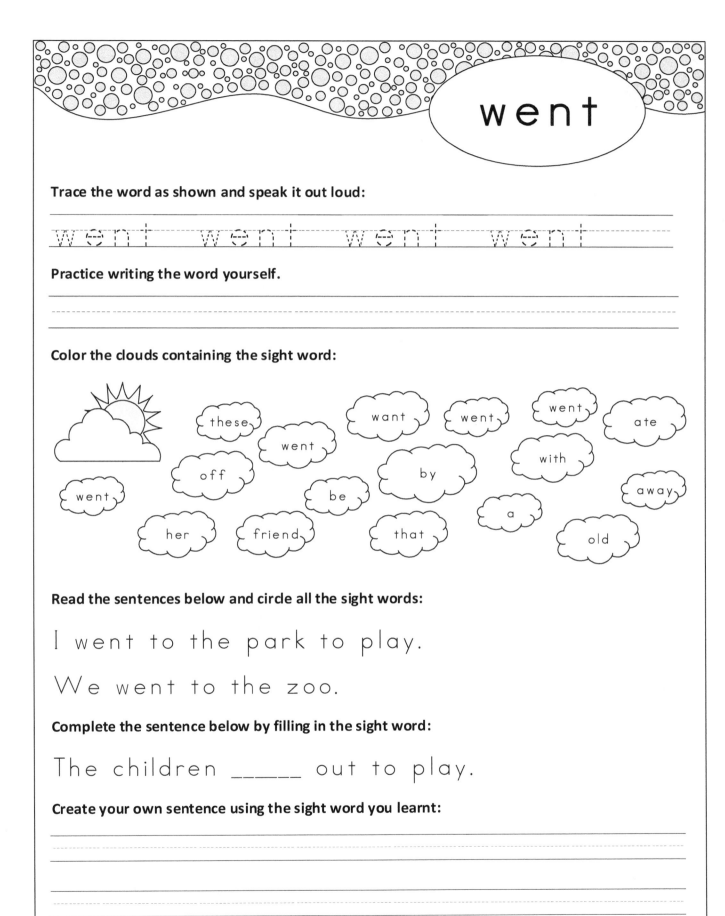

Read the sentences below and circle all the sight words:

I went to the park to play.

We went to the zoo.

Complete the sentence below by filling in the sight word:

The children _____ out to play.

Create your own sentence using the sight word you learnt:

that

Trace the word as shown and speak it out loud:

that that that that

Practice writing the word yourself.

Color the clouds containing the sight word:

help
she
ate
when
or
one
that
my
they
that
up
that
eat
that
that
push
with
some

Read the sentences below and circle all the sight words:

I love that red car.

Who is that boy?

Complete the sentence below by filling in the sight word:

Look at _____ big elephant!

Create your own sentence using the sight word you learnt:

they

Trace the word as shown and speak it out loud:

they   they   they   they

Practice writing the word yourself.

Color the clouds containing the sight word:

Read the sentences below and circle all the sight words:

I played with my friends when they came.

They are my friends.

Complete the sentence below by filling in the sight word:

_____ have a lot of books.

Create your own sentence using the sight word you learnt:

away

Trace the word as shown and speak it out loud:

away   away   away   away

Practice writing the word yourself.

Color the clouds containing the sight word:

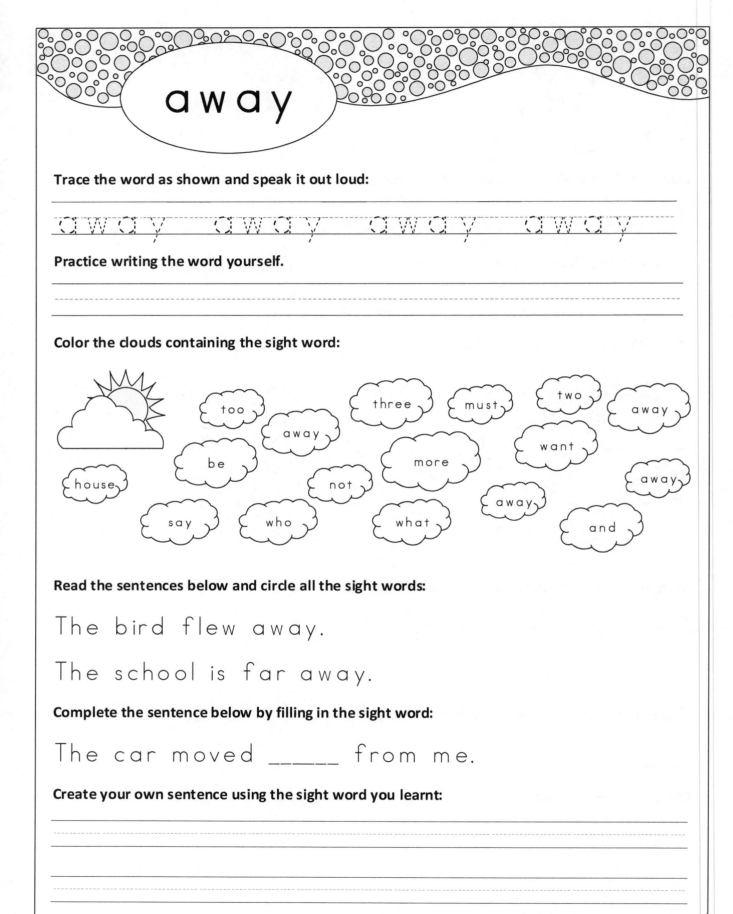

too
away
three   must   two   away
be   want
more
house   not   away
say   who   what   and

Read the sentences below and circle all the sight words:

The bird flew away.

The school is far away.

Complete the sentence below by filling in the sight word:

The car moved _____ from me.

Create your own sentence using the sight word you learnt:

must

Trace the word as shown and speak it out loud:

must   must   must   must

Practice writing the word yourself.

Color the clouds containing the sight word:

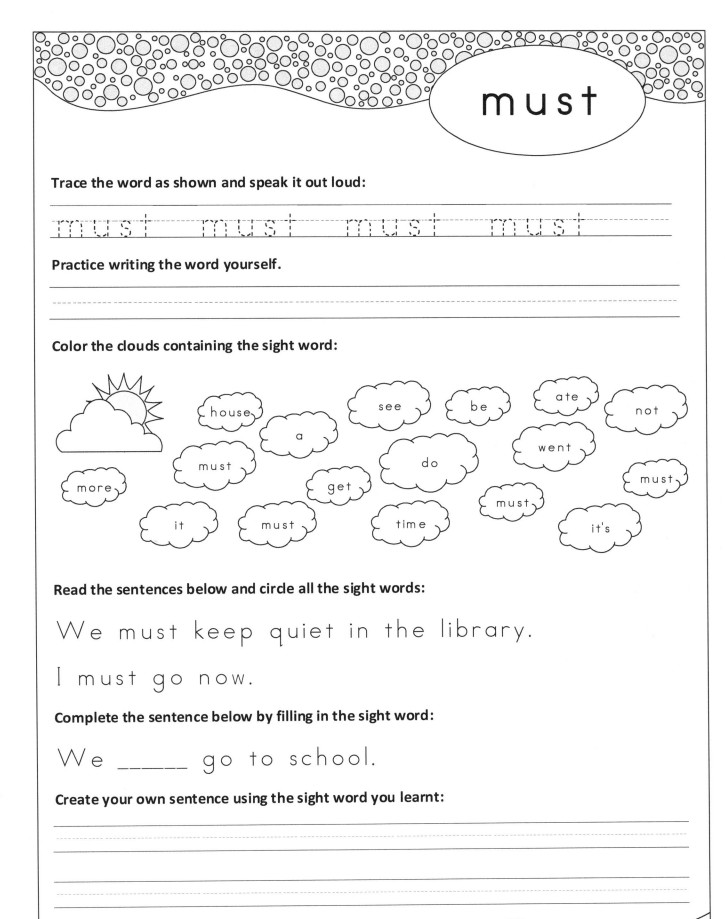

house   see   be   ate   not

a   must   went

more   do   must

get   must

it   must   time   it's

Read the sentences below and circle all the sight words:

We must keep quiet in the library.

I must go now.

Complete the sentence below by filling in the sight word:

We _____ go to school.

Create your own sentence using the sight word you learnt:

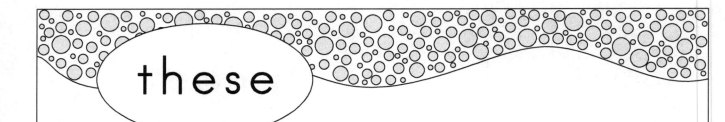

these

Trace the word as shown and speak it out loud:

t͟h͟e͟s͟e͟   t͟h͟e͟s͟e͟   t͟h͟e͟s͟e͟

Practice writing the word yourself.

Color the clouds containing the sight word:

Read the sentences below and circle all the sight words:

These books are from the library.

Can you throw these papers away?

Complete the sentence below by filling in the sight word:

_____ flowers are beautiful.

Create your own sentence using the sight word you learnt:

this

Trace the word as shown and speak it out loud:

this   this   this   this   this

Practice writing the word yourself.

Color the clouds containing the sight word:

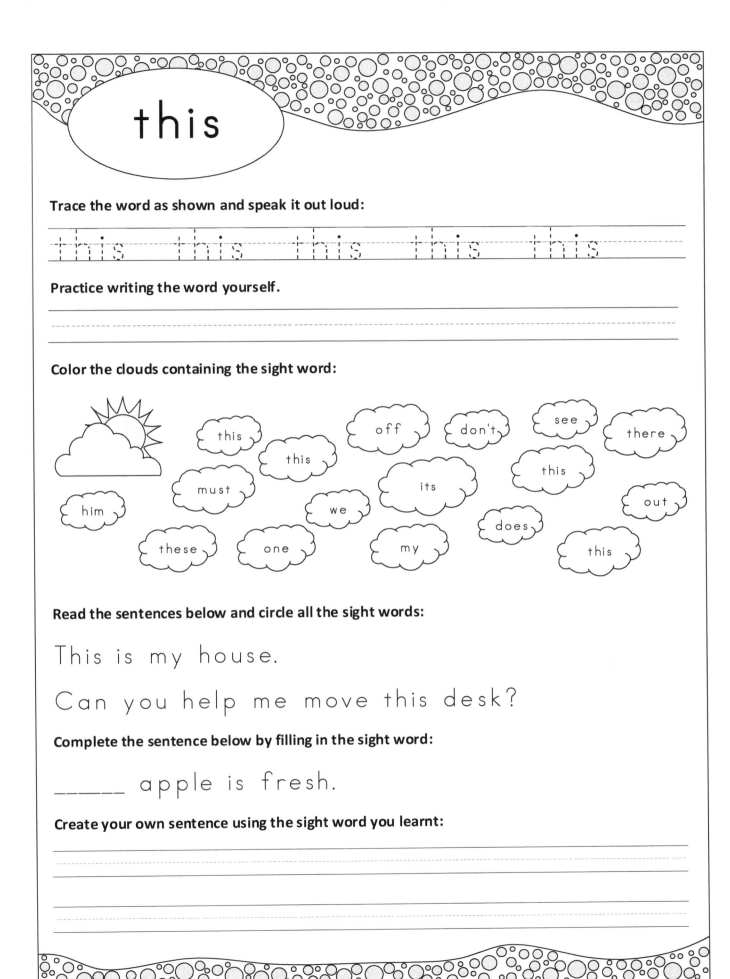

this this off don't see there
must its this
him we out
these one my does this

Read the sentences below and circle all the sight words:

This is my house.

Can you help me move this desk?

Complete the sentence below by filling in the sight word:

_____ apple is fresh.

Create your own sentence using the sight word you learnt:

live

Trace the word as shown and speak it out loud:

live   live   live   live   live

Practice writing the word yourself.

Color the clouds containing the sight word:

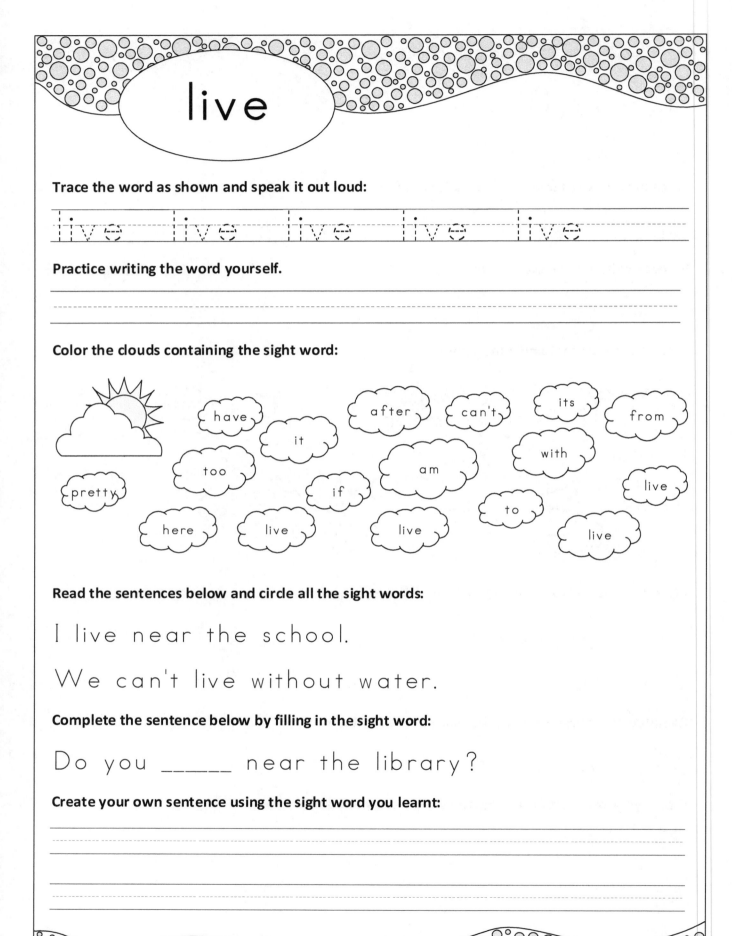

have
it
after
can't
its
from
too
am
with
pretty
if
live
here
live
live
to
live

Read the sentences below and circle all the sight words:

I live near the school.

We can't live without water.

Complete the sentence below by filling in the sight word:

Do you _____ near the library?

Create your own sentence using the sight word you learnt:

from

Trace the word as shown and speak it out loud:

from   from   from   from

Practice writing the word yourself.

Color the clouds containing the sight word:

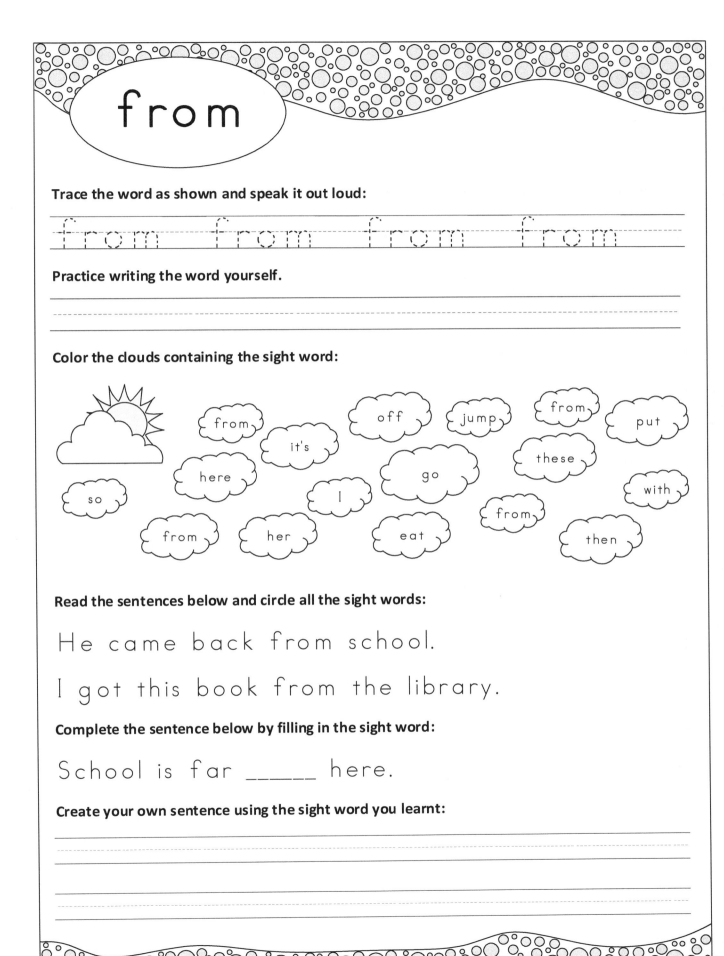

Read the sentences below and circle all the sight words:

He came back from school.

I got this book from the library.

Complete the sentence below by filling in the sight word:

School is far _____ here.

Create your own sentence using the sight word you learnt:

s a w

Trace the word as shown and speak it out loud:

saw   saw   saw   saw   saw

Practice writing the word yourself.

Color the clouds containing the sight word:

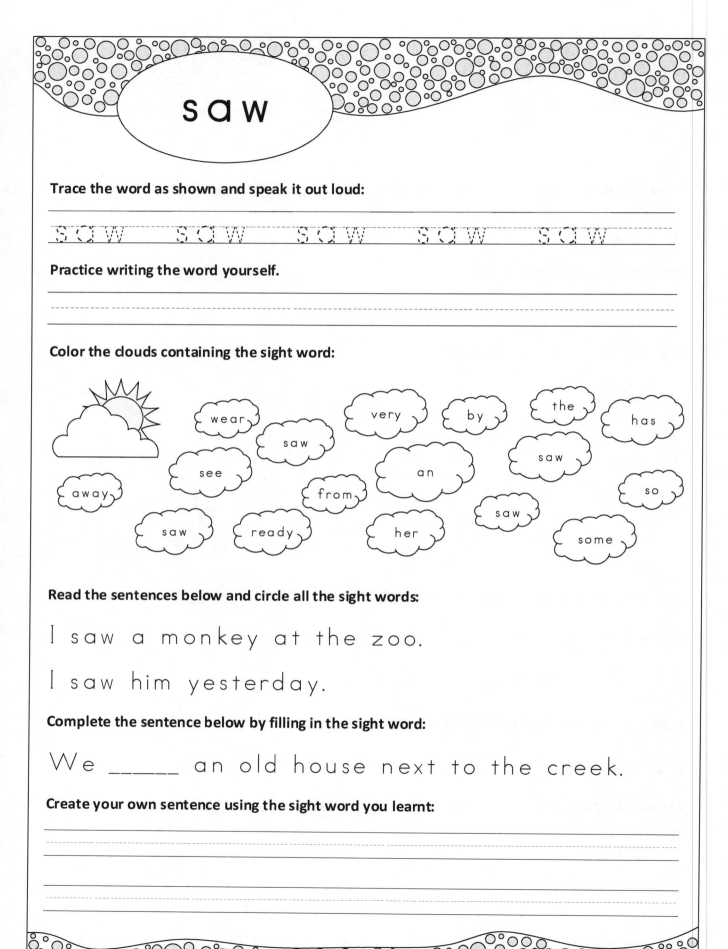

Read the sentences below and circle all the sight words:

I saw a monkey at the zoo.

I saw him yesterday.

Complete the sentence below by filling in the sight word:

We _____ an old house next to the creek.

Create your own sentence using the sight word you learnt:

say

Trace the word as shown and speak it out loud:

say   say   say   say   say

Practice writing the word yourself.

Color the clouds containing the sight word:

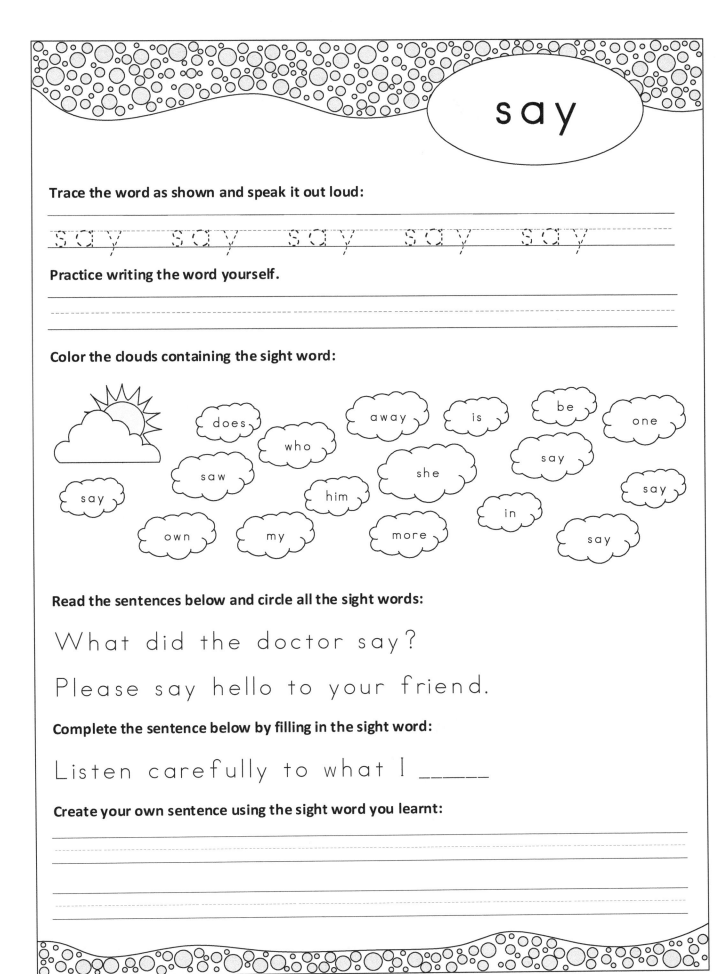

does   away   is   be   one

who

saw   she   say

say   him   say

own   my   more   in   say

Read the sentences below and circle all the sight words:

What did the doctor say?

Please say hello to your friend.

Complete the sentence below by filling in the sight word:

Listen carefully to what I _____

Create your own sentence using the sight word you learnt:

those

Trace the word as shown and speak it out loud:

those   those   those

Practice writing the word yourself.

Color the clouds containing the sight word:

off   where   those   go   push   those   at   in   pretty   for   it   those   after   from   was   ate   those   those

Read the sentences below and circle all the sight words:

Those are my toys.

Those flowers are beautiful.

Complete the sentence below by filling in the sight word:

Can you read _____ books?

Create your own sentence using the sight word you learnt:

it's

Trace the word as shown and speak it out loud:

it's   it's   it's   it's   it's   it's

Practice writing the word yourself.

Color the clouds containing the sight word:

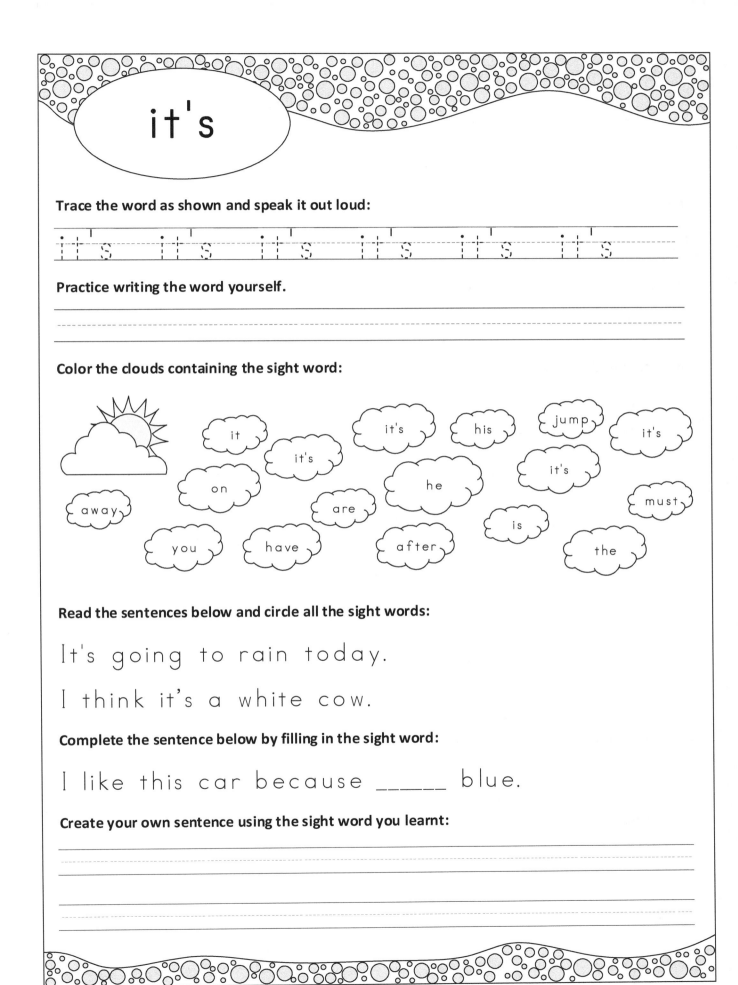

Read the sentences below and circle all the sight words:

It's going to rain today.

I think it's a white cow.

Complete the sentence below by filling in the sight word:

I like this car because _____ blue.

Create your own sentence using the sight word you learnt:

have

Trace the word as shown and speak it out loud:

have   have   have   have

Practice writing the word yourself.

Color the clouds containing the sight word:

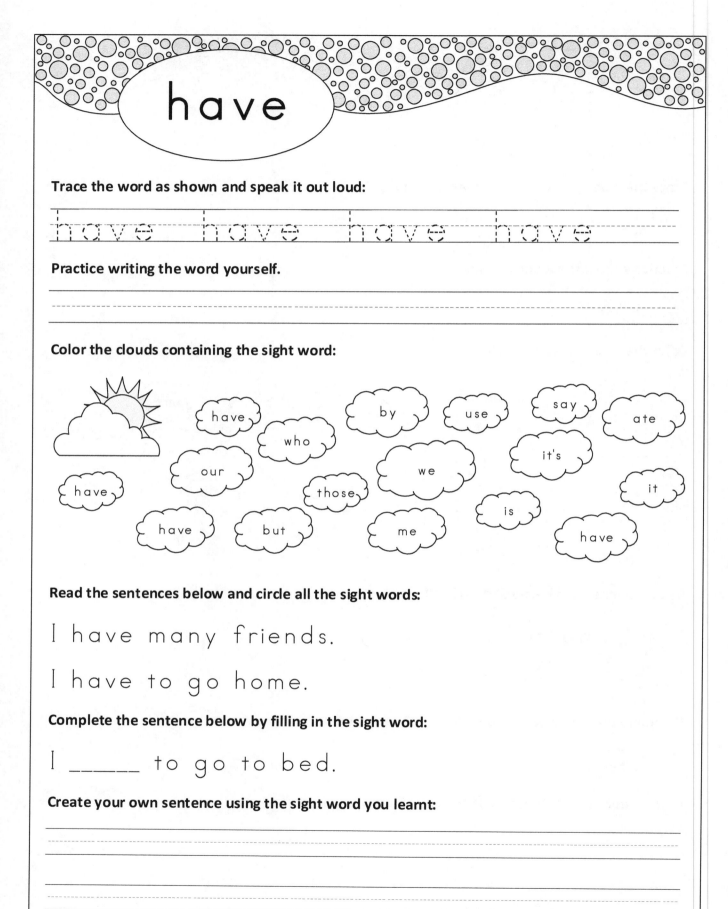

have   by   use   say   ate
who
our   we   it's
have   those   it
have   but   me   is   have

Read the sentences below and circle all the sight words:

I have many friends.

I have to go home.

Complete the sentence below by filling in the sight word:

I _____ to go to bed.

Create your own sentence using the sight word you learnt:

here

Trace the word as shown and speak it out loud:

here here here here

Practice writing the word yourself.

Color the clouds containing the sight word:

can't here by help here you

own here on

do up very

it here but an out

Read the sentences below and circle all the sight words:

I eat here, on this table.

Can you please come here?

Complete the sentence below by filling in the sight word:

My school is far from _____

Create your own sentence using the sight word you learnt:

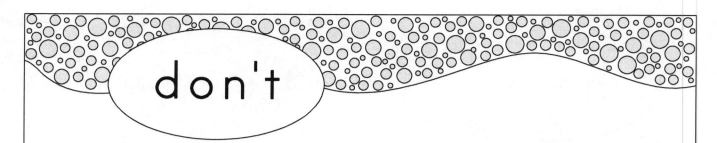

don't

Trace the word as shown and speak it out loud:

don't   don't   don't   don't

Practice writing the word yourself.

_____

- -

Color the clouds containing the sight word:

Read the sentences below and circle all the sight words:

I don't need a new pencil.

I don't know how to play the piano.

Complete the sentence below by filling in the sight word:

_____ touch the hot coffee mug.

Create your own sentence using the sight word you learnt:

_____

- -

_____

_____

- -

like

Trace the word as shown and speak it out loud:

like   like   like   like   like

Practice writing the word yourself.

Color the clouds containing the sight word:

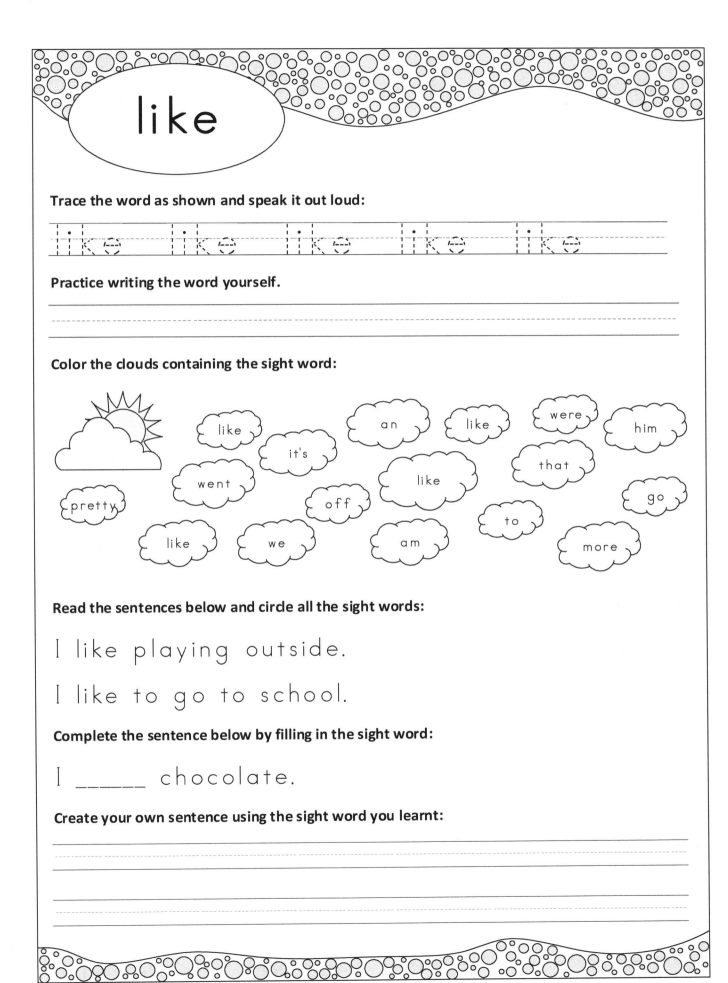

Read the sentences below and circle all the sight words:

I like playing outside.

I like to go to school.

Complete the sentence below by filling in the sight word:

I _____ chocolate.

Create your own sentence using the sight word you learnt:

out

Trace the word as shown and speak it out loud:

out   out   out   out   out

Practice writing the word yourself.

Color the clouds containing the sight word:

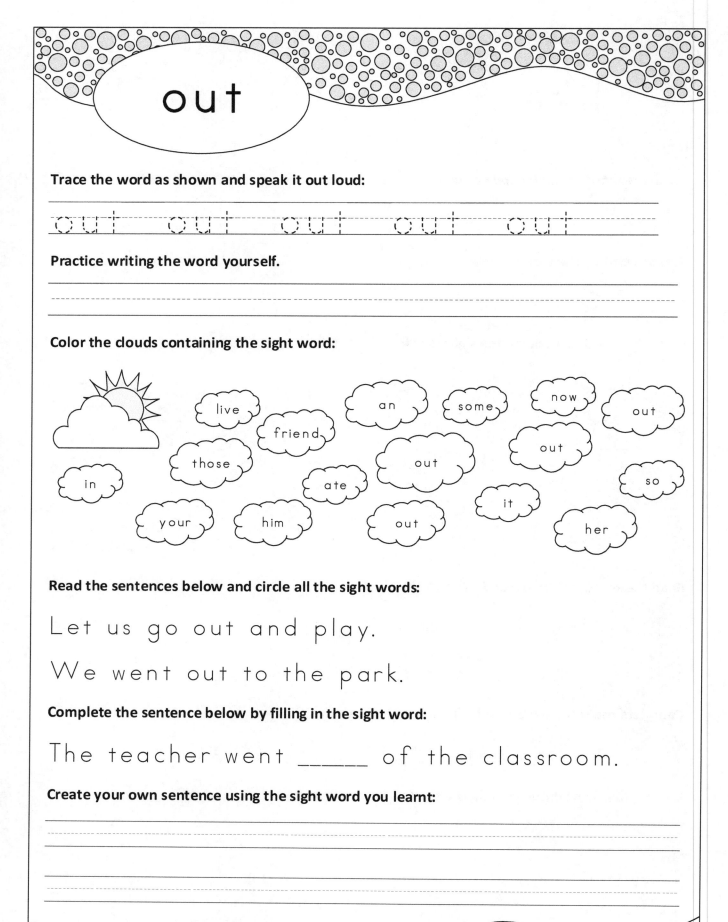

live an some now out
friend
those out out
in ate so
it
your him out her

Read the sentences below and circle all the sight words:

Let us go out and play.

We went out to the park.

Complete the sentence below by filling in the sight word:

The teacher went _____ of the classroom.

Create your own sentence using the sight word you learnt:

was

Trace the word as shown and speak it out loud:

was   was   was   was   was

Practice writing the word yourself.

Color the clouds containing the sight word:

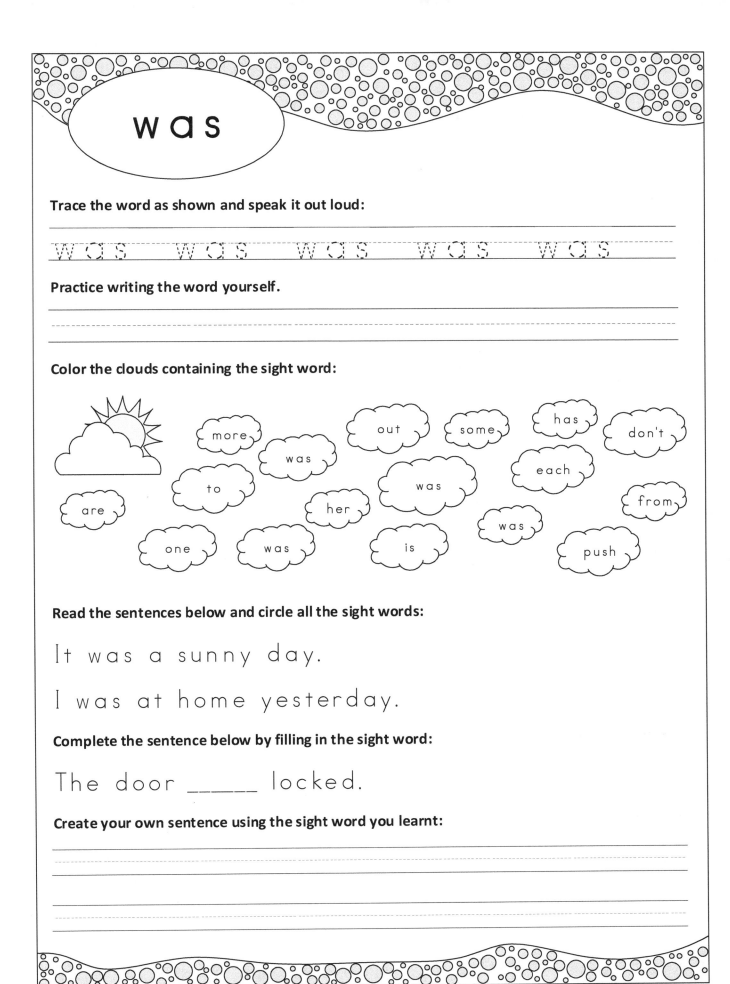

more   was   out   some   has   don't
        was   each
    to   was   from
are   was
    one   was   is   push   her

Read the sentences below and circle all the sight words:

It was a sunny day.

I was at home yesterday.

Complete the sentence below by filling in the sight word:

The door _____ locked.

Create your own sentence using the sight word you learnt:

does

Trace the word as shown and speak it out loud:

does   does   does   does

Practice writing the word yourself.

Color the clouds containing the sight word:

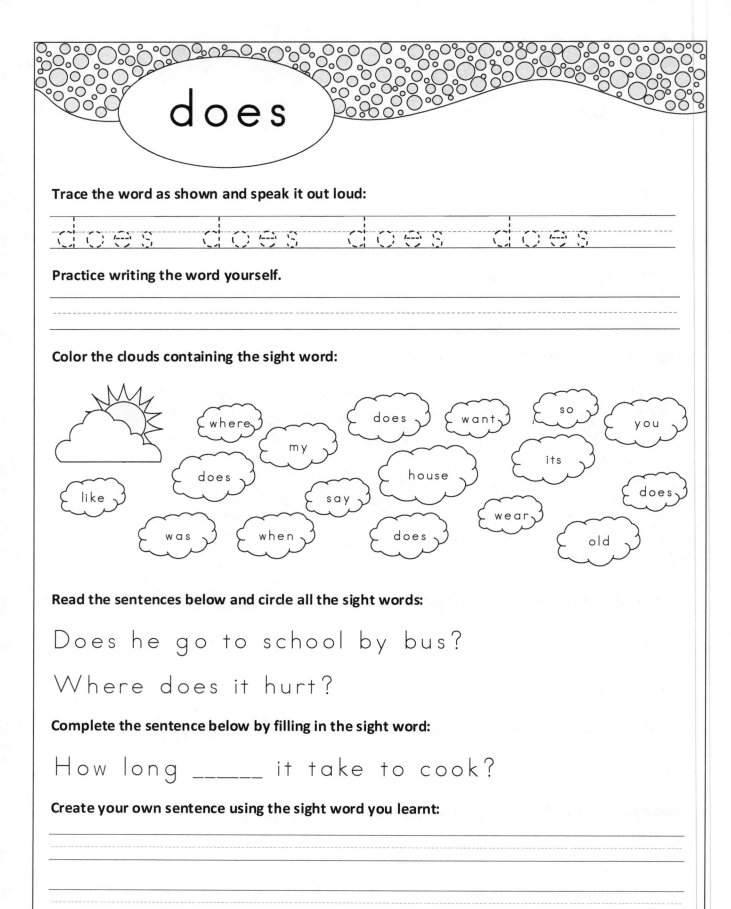

where   does   want   so   you

my   its

does   house

like   say   does

wear

was   when   does   old

Read the sentences below and circle all the sight words:

Does he go to school by bus?

Where does it hurt?

Complete the sentence below by filling in the sight word:

How long _____ it take to cook?

Create your own sentence using the sight word you learnt:

n o w

Trace the word as shown and speak it out loud:

n o w   n o w   n o w   n o w

Practice writing the word yourself.

Color the clouds containing the sight word:

Read the sentences below and circle all the sight words:

I have to go to bed now.

Please do your homework now.

Complete the sentence below by filling in the sight word:

It's _____ my turn.

Create your own sentence using the sight word you learnt:

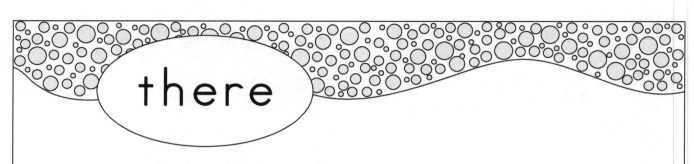

there

Trace the word as shown and speak it out loud:

there   there   there

Practice writing the word yourself.

Color the clouds containing the sight word:

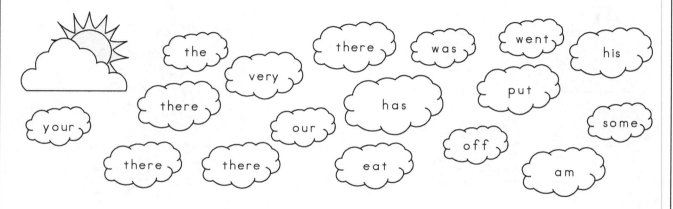

Read the sentences below and circle all the sight words:

The zoo is not far, I want to go there.

No one was there at the park.

Complete the sentence below by filling in the sight word:

_____ is a slide at the park.

Create your own sentence using the sight word you learnt:

My First Workbook of 100 Sight Words

time

Trace the word as shown and speak it out loud:

time   time   time   time

Practice writing the word yourself.

Color the clouds containing the sight word:

Read the sentences below and circle all the sight words:

It's time for bed.

I need more time to play.

Complete the sentence below by filling in the sight word:

The bus arrived in _____

Create your own sentence using the sight word you learnt:

more

Trace the word as shown and speak it out loud:

more   more   more   more

Practice writing the word yourself.

Color the clouds containing the sight word:

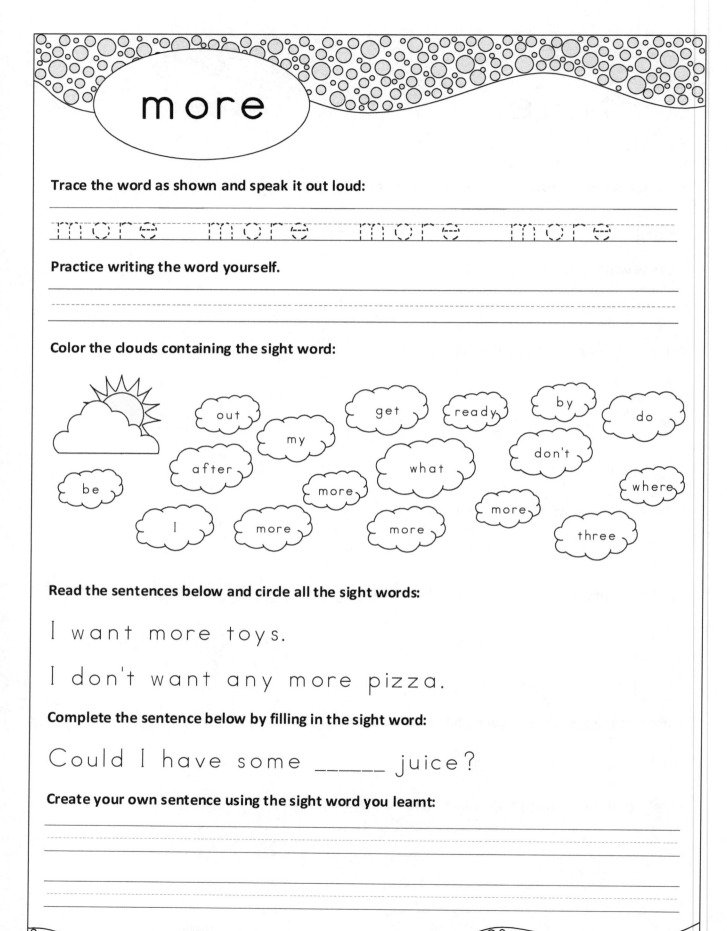

out   my   get   ready   by   do
after   what   don't
be   more   more   where
I   more   more   more   three

Read the sentences below and circle all the sight words:

I want more toys.

I don't want any more pizza.

Complete the sentence below by filling in the sight word:

Could I have some _____ juice?

Create your own sentence using the sight word you learnt:

each

Trace the word as shown and speak it out loud:

each   each   each   each

Practice writing the word yourself.

Color the clouds containing the sight word:

Read the sentences below and circle all the sight words:

Brush your teeth after each meal.

We should help each other.

Complete the sentence below by filling in the sight word:

Read a story _____ day.

Create your own sentence using the sight word you learnt:

were

Trace the word as shown and speak it out loud:

were   were   were   were

Practice writing the word yourself.

Color the clouds containing the sight word:

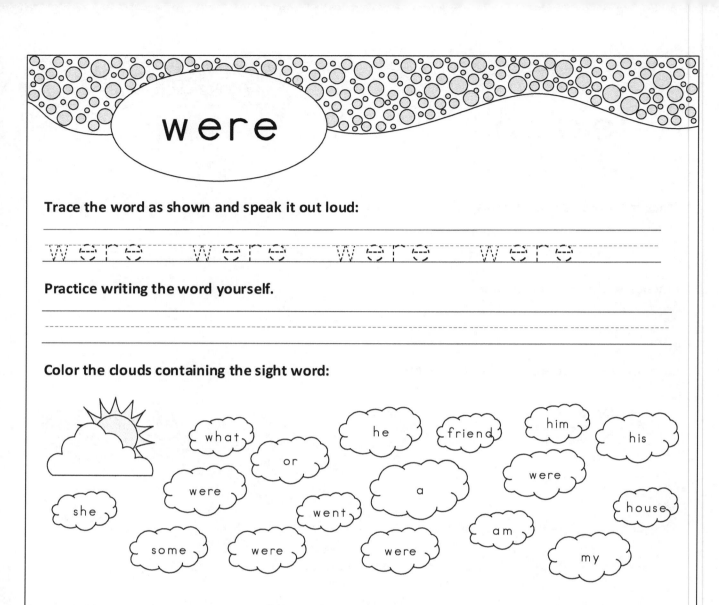

Read the sentences below and circle all the sight words:

We were quiet in the library.

There were two slices of pizza left.

Complete the sentence below by filling in the sight word:

Kids _____ playing soccer.

Create your own sentence using the sight word you learnt:

very

Trace the word as shown and speak it out loud:

very   very   very   very

Practice writing the word yourself.

Color the clouds containing the sight word:

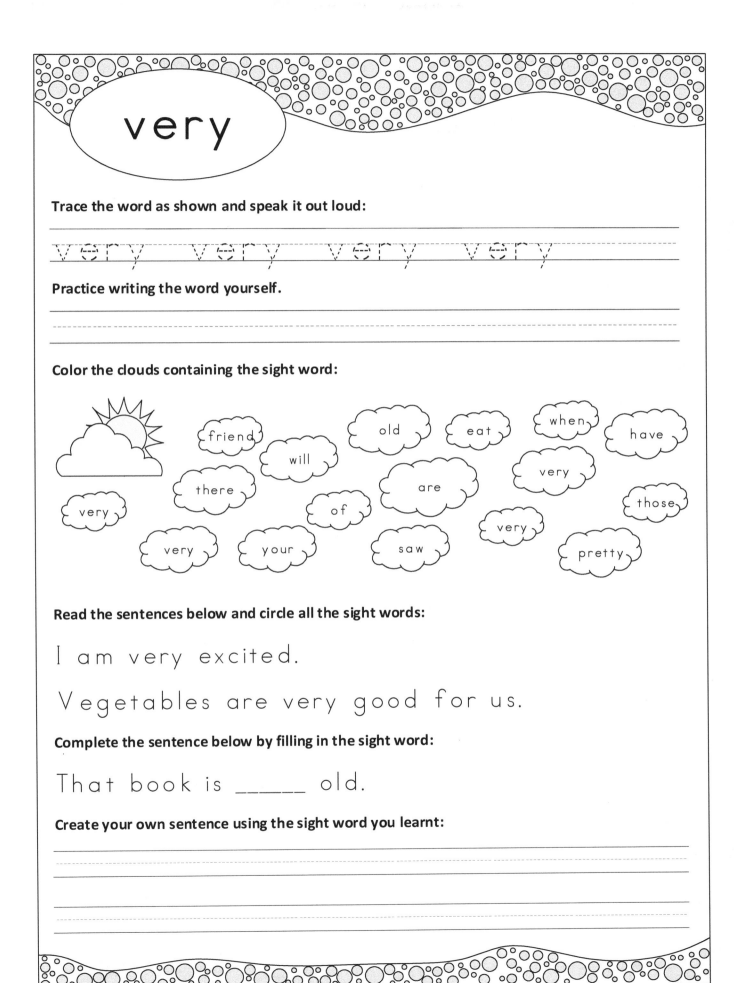

friend   old   eat   when   have
will
there   are   very
of   very
very   very   those
very   your   saw   pretty

Read the sentences below and circle all the sight words:

I am very excited.

Vegetables are very good for us.

Complete the sentence below by filling in the sight word:

That book is _____ old.

Create your own sentence using the sight word you learnt:

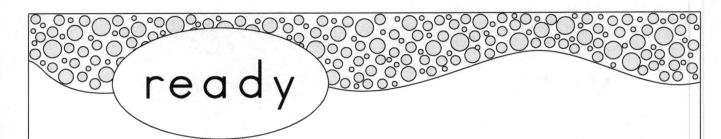

ready

Trace the word as shown and speak it out loud:

ready   ready   ready

Practice writing the word yourself.

Color the clouds containing the sight word:

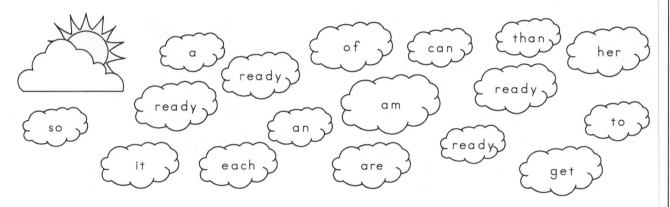

Read the sentences below and circle all the sight words:

I am ready for school.

Are you ready?

Complete the sentence below by filling in the sight word:

Dinner is _____

Create your own sentence using the sight word you learnt:

My First Workbook of 100 Sight Words

some

Trace the word as shown and speak it out loud:

some   some   some   some

Practice writing the word yourself.

Color the clouds containing the sight word:

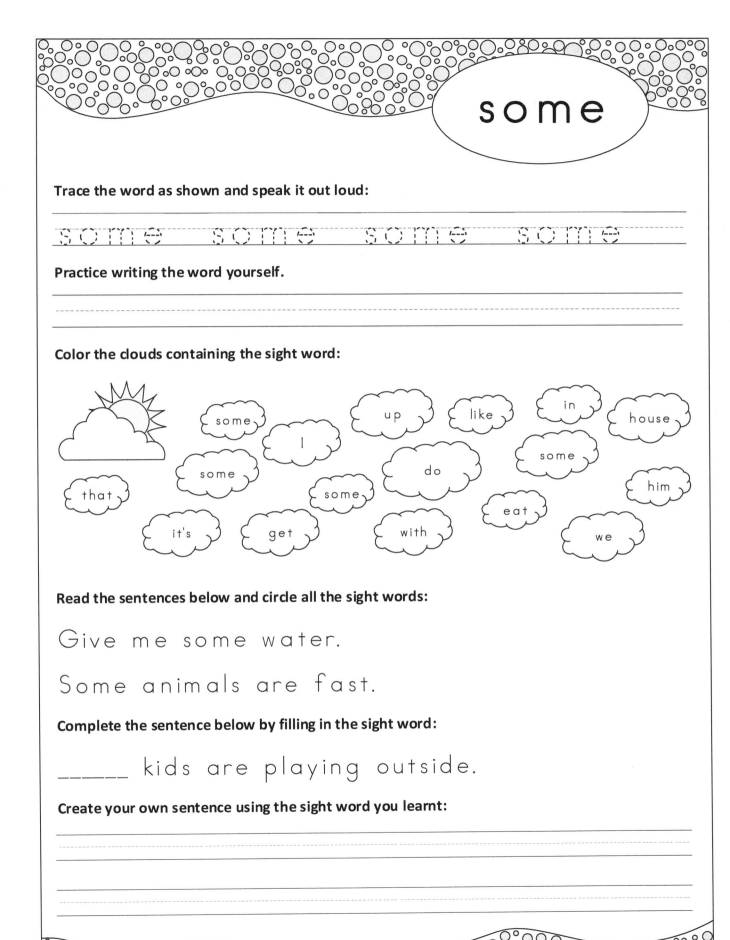

some   up   like   in   house

I   some

some

that   some   do   him

it's   get   with   eat   we

Read the sentences below and circle all the sight words:

Give me some water.

Some animals are fast.

Complete the sentence below by filling in the sight word:

_____ kids are playing outside.

Create your own sentence using the sight word you learnt:

than

Trace the word as shown and speak it out loud:

than   than   than   than

Practice writing the word yourself.

Color the clouds containing the sight word:

not   a   than   time   want   in
does   the   than
please   old   than
than   go   was   now   push

Read the sentences below and circle all the sight words:

I am taller than him.

The elephant is bigger than the horse.

Complete the sentence below by filling in the sight word:

The turtle is slower _____ the bunny.

Create your own sentence using the sight word you learnt:

wear

Trace the word as shown and speak it out loud:

wear   wear   wear   wear

Practice writing the word yourself.

Color the clouds containing the sight word:

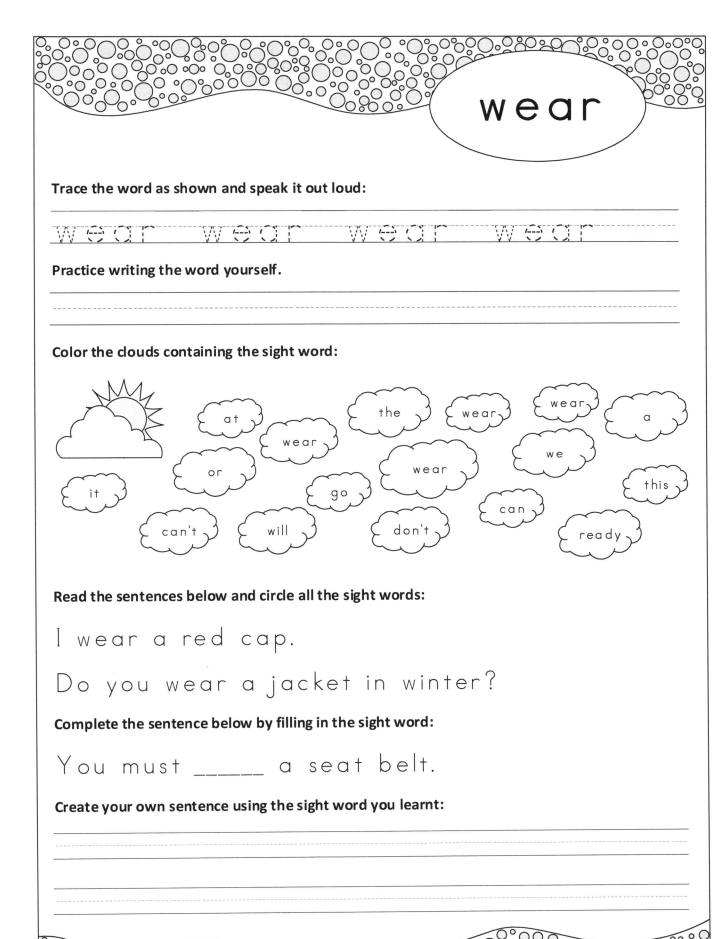

at
wear
the   wear   wear   a
or   wear   we
it   go   this
can't   will   don't   can   ready

Read the sentences below and circle all the sight words:

I wear a red cap.

Do you wear a jacket in winter?

Complete the sentence below by filling in the sight word:

You must _____ a seat belt.

Create your own sentence using the sight word you learnt:

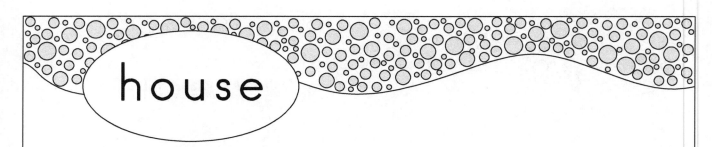

house

Trace the word as shown and speak it out loud:

house   house   house

Practice writing the word yourself.

Color the clouds containing the sight word:

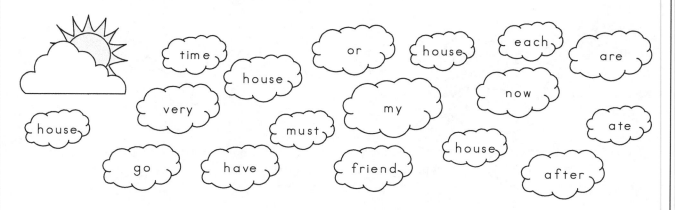

Read the sentences below and circle all the sight words:

Their house is new.

My house is painted green.

Complete the sentence below by filling in the sight word:

I let my dog out of the _____

Create your own sentence using the sight word you learnt:

after

Trace the word as shown and speak it out loud:

after   after   after

Practice writing the word yourself.

Color the clouds containing the sight word:

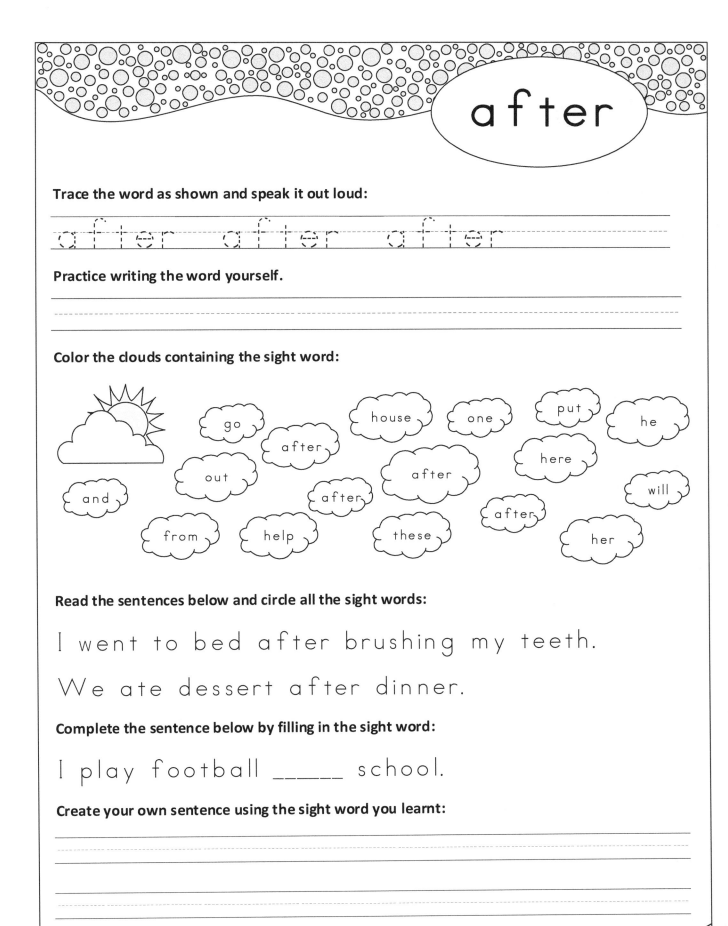

go

after

house   one   put   he

out

here

and

after   after   will

from   help   after   these   her

Read the sentences below and circle all the sight words:

I went to bed after brushing my teeth.

We ate dessert after dinner.

Complete the sentence below by filling in the sight word:

I play football _____ school.

Create your own sentence using the sight word you learnt:

ate

Trace the word as shown and speak it out loud:

ate   ate   ate   ate   ate

Practice writing the word yourself.

Color the clouds containing the sight word:

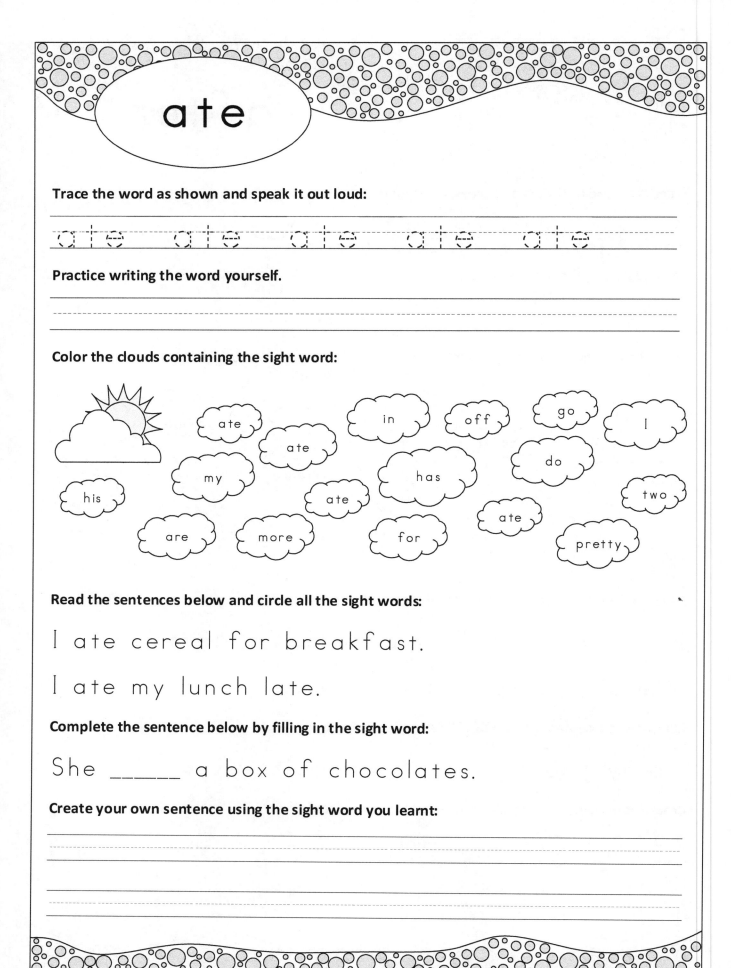

Read the sentences below and circle all the sight words:

I ate cereal for breakfast.

I ate my lunch late.

Complete the sentence below by filling in the sight word:

She _____ a box of chocolates.

Create your own sentence using the sight word you learnt:

where

Trace the word as shown and speak it out loud:

where   where   where

Practice writing the word yourself.

Color the clouds containing the sight word:

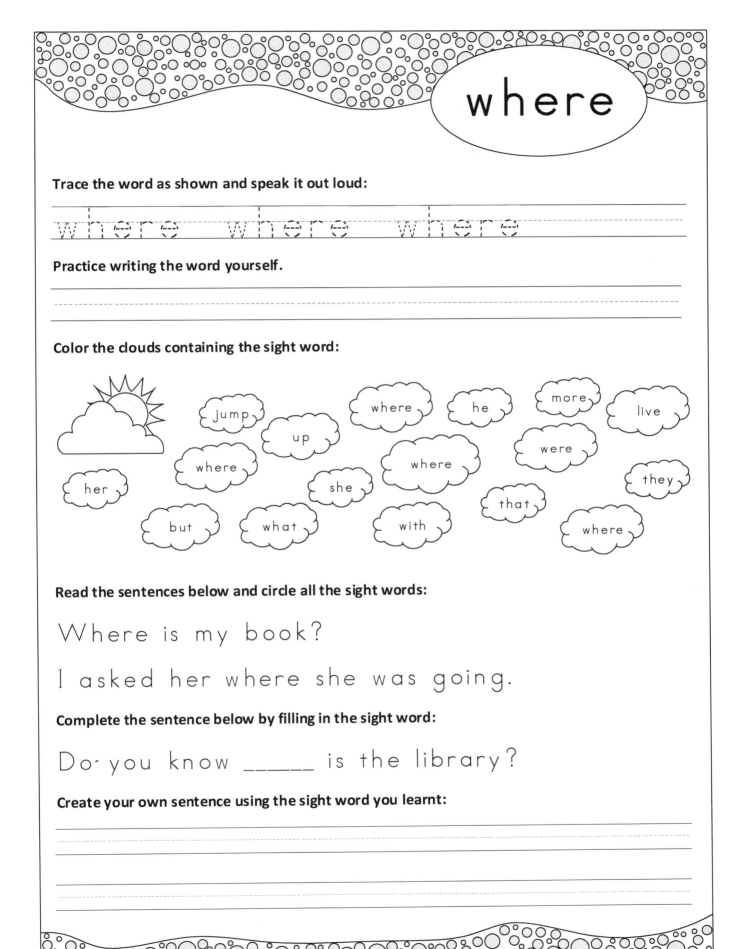

jump   where   he   more   live

where   up   were

her   where   she   that   they

but   what   with   where

Read the sentences below and circle all the sight words:

Where is my book?

I asked her where she was going.

Complete the sentence below by filling in the sight word:

Do you know _____ is the library?

Create your own sentence using the sight word you learnt:

please

Trace the word as shown and speak it out loud:

please   please   please

Practice writing the word yourself.

Color the clouds containing the sight word:

please   like   from   am   went

don't   please

those   use   will

at   please

please   to   then   that   who

Read the sentences below and circle all the sight words:

Please come and play with me.

Wait in line, please.

Complete the sentence below by filling in the sight word:

Will you _____ help me?

Create your own sentence using the sight word you learnt:

My First Workbook of 100 Sight Words

use

Trace the word as shown and speak it out loud:

use   use   use   use   use

Practice writing the word yourself.

Color the clouds containing the sight word:

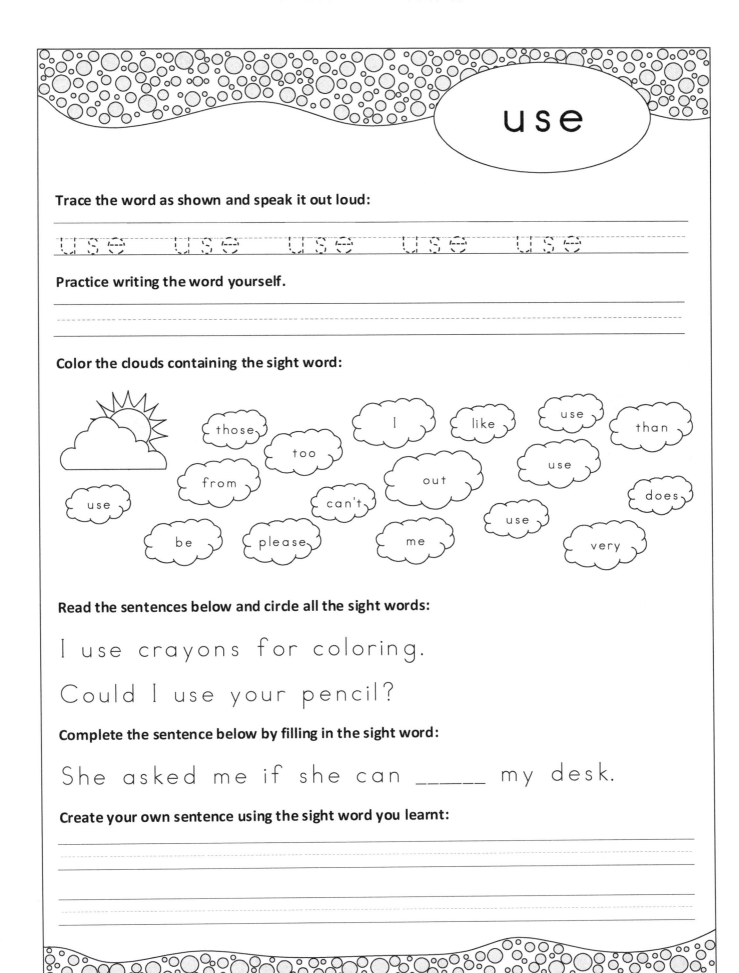

those   too   I   like   use   than
from   out   use
use   can't   does
be   please   me   use   very

Read the sentences below and circle all the sight words:

I use crayons for coloring.

Could I use your pencil?

Complete the sentence below by filling in the sight word:

She asked me if she can _____ my desk.

Create your own sentence using the sight word you learnt:

own

Trace the word as shown and speak it out loud:

own   own   own   own

Practice writing the word yourself.

Color the clouds containing the sight word:

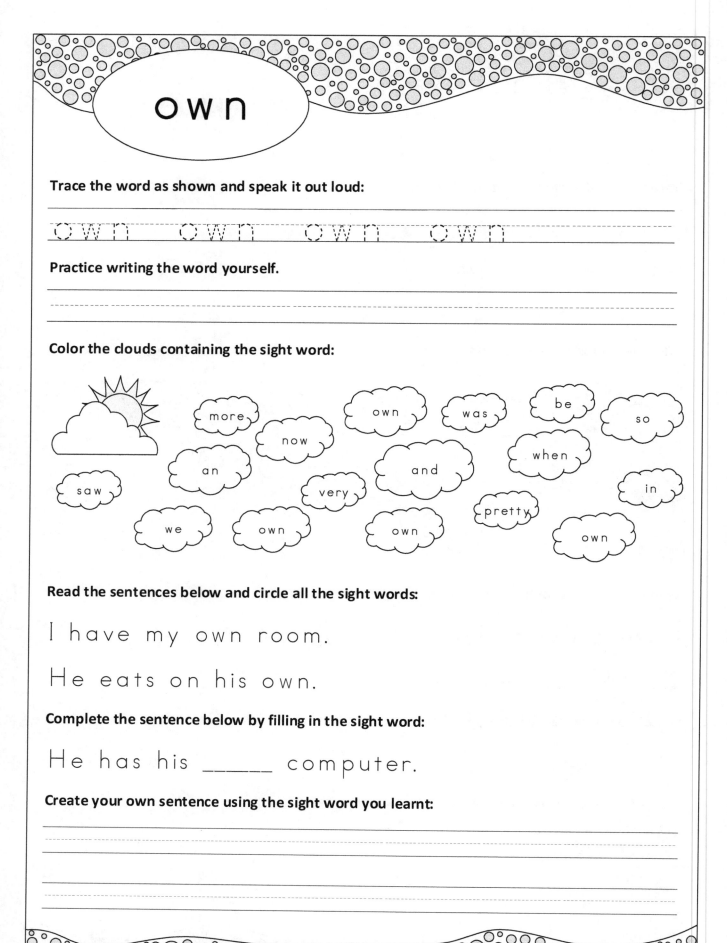

more
now
an
saw
we
own
very
own
own
was
be
so
when
and
pretty
in
own

Read the sentences below and circle all the sight words:

I have my own room.

He eats on his own.

Complete the sentence below by filling in the sight word:

He has his _____ computer.

Create your own sentence using the sight word you learnt:

two

Trace the word as shown and speak it out loud:

two   two   two   two   two

Practice writing the word yourself.

Color the clouds containing the sight word:

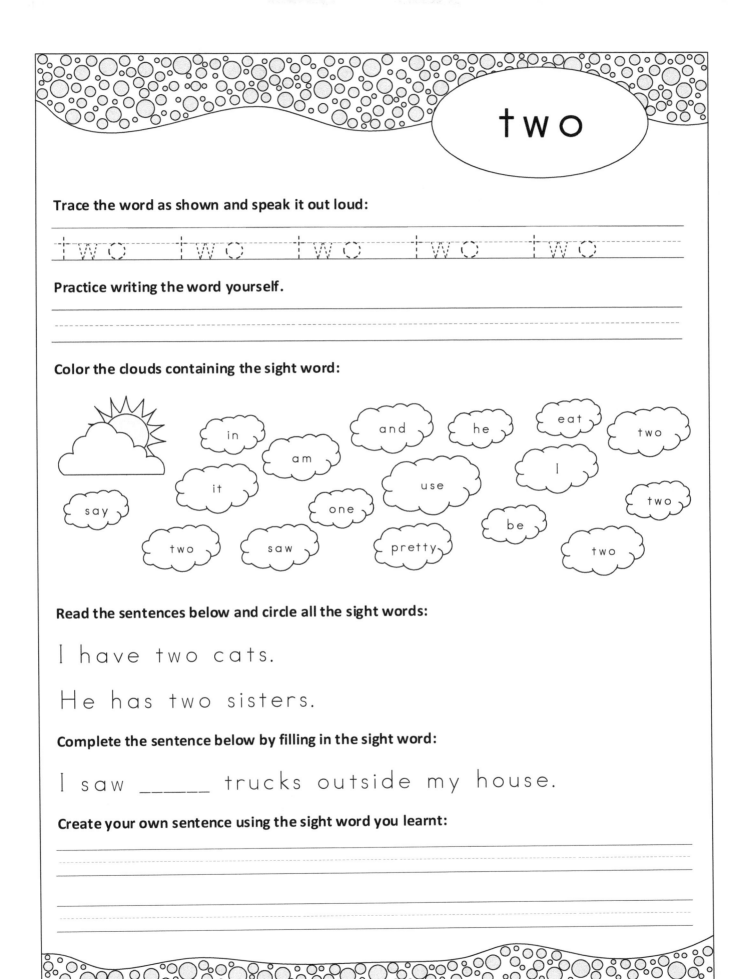

in   am   and   he   eat   two

it   use   I

say   one   two

two   saw   be

pretty   two

Read the sentences below and circle all the sight words:

I have two cats.

He has two sisters.

Complete the sentence below by filling in the sight word:

I saw _____ trucks outside my house.

Create your own sentence using the sight word you learnt:

then

Trace the word as shown and speak it out loud:

then   then   then   then

Practice writing the word yourself.

Color the clouds containing the sight word:

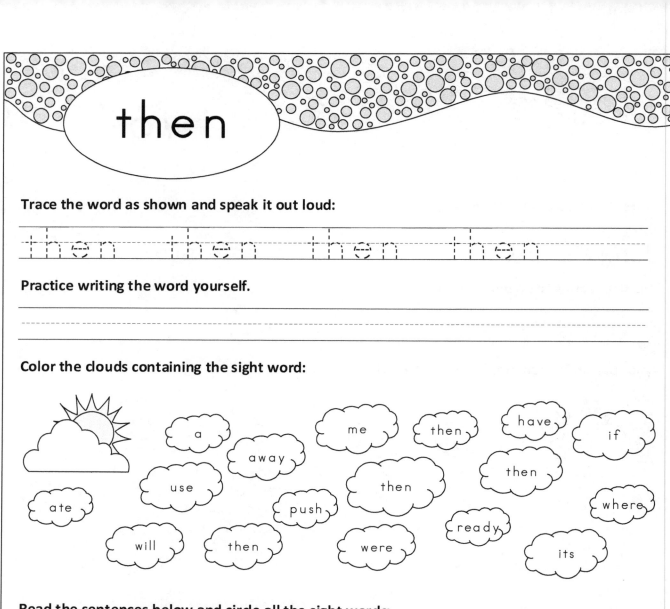

a
away
me
then
have
if
use
then
then
ate
push
where
push
will
then
were
ready
its

Read the sentences below and circle all the sight words:

I ate a burger then went for a walk.

She ate a donut, then took another one.

Complete the sentence below by filling in the sight word:

He took the book, _____ left.

Create your own sentence using the sight word you learnt:

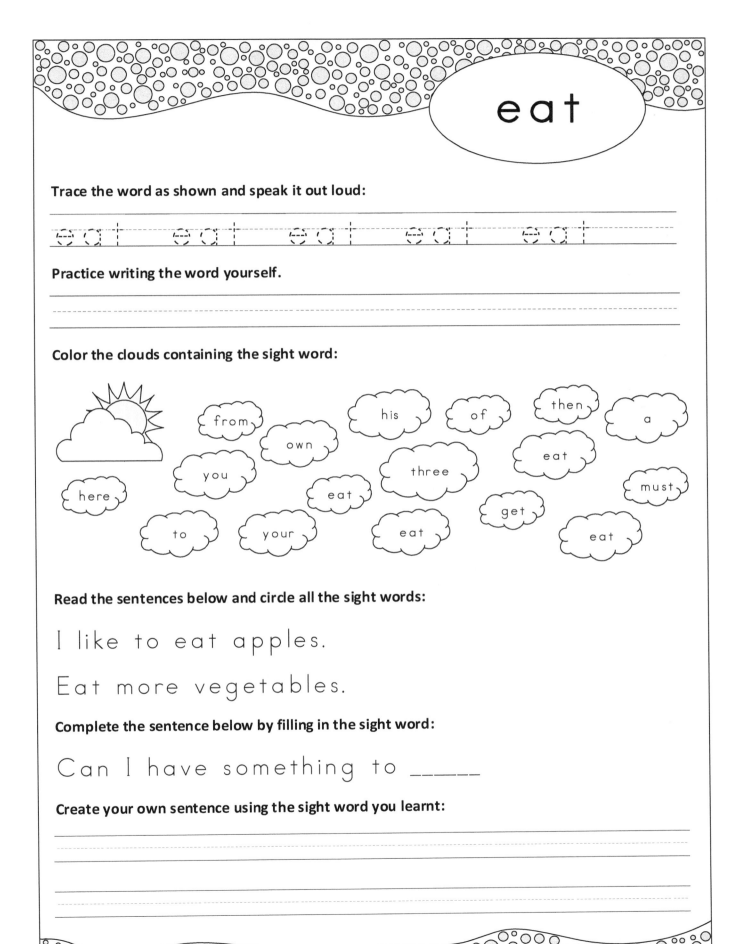

eat

Trace the word as shown and speak it out loud:

eat   eat   eat   eat   eat

Practice writing the word yourself.

Color the clouds containing the sight word:

from   his   of   then   a

own

you   three   eat

here   eat   must

to   your   eat   get

eat

Read the sentences below and circle all the sight words:

I like to eat apples.

Eat more vegetables.

Complete the sentence below by filling in the sight word:

Can I have something to _____

Create your own sentence using the sight word you learnt:

jump

Trace the word as shown and speak it out loud:

jump   jump   jump   jump

Practice writing the word yourself.

Color the clouds containing the sight word:

some · like · jump · push · my
jump
who · is · I · that
for · wear
a · where · can't · jump · jump

Read the sentences below and circle all the sight words:

She can jump high.

He made the squirrel jump off the tree.

Complete the sentence below by filling in the sight word:

I _____ when I am excited.

Create your own sentence using the sight word you learnt:

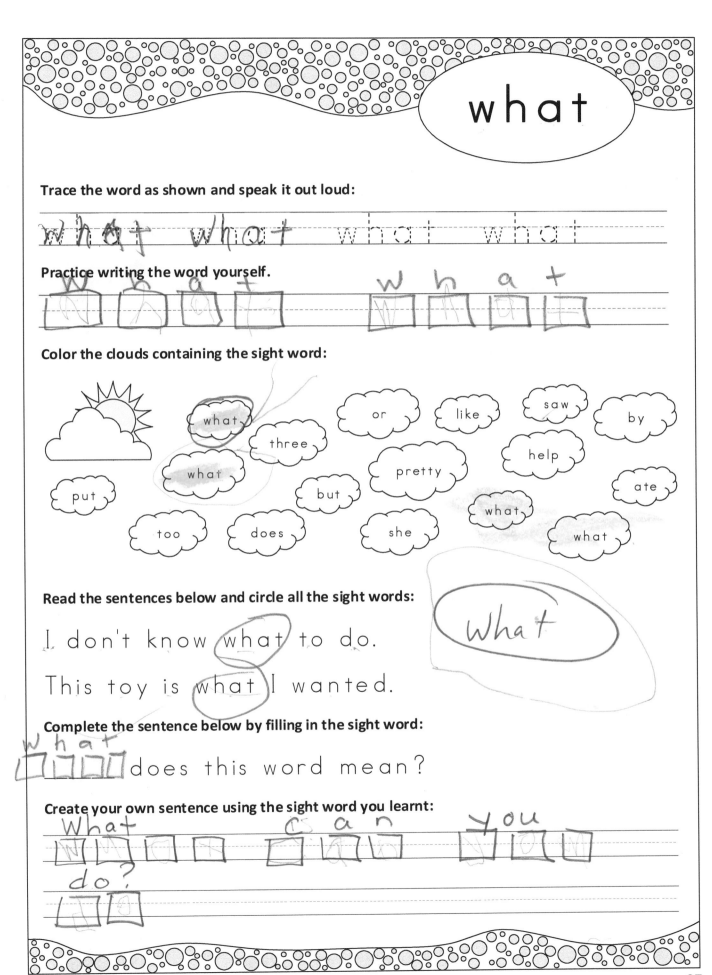

what

Trace the word as shown and speak it out loud:

what   what   what   what

Practice writing the word yourself.

Color the clouds containing the sight word:

what
three
what
put
or
like
saw
by
help
pretty
ate
but
what
too
does
she
what

Read the sentences below and circle all the sight words:

I don't know (what) to do.

This toy is (what) I wanted.

What

Complete the sentence below by filling in the sight word:

what does this word mean?

Create your own sentence using the sight word you learnt:

What can you do?

can't

Trace the word as shown and speak it out loud:

can't   can't   can't   can't

Practice writing the word yourself.

Color the clouds containing the sight word:

Read the sentences below and circle all the sight words:

I can't hear it.

Penguins can't fly.

Complete the sentence below by filling in the sight word:

I _____ eat anymore donuts.

Create your own sentence using the sight word you learnt:

pretty

Trace the word as shown and speak it out loud:

pretty   pretty   pretty

Practice writing the word yourself.

Color the clouds containing the sight word:

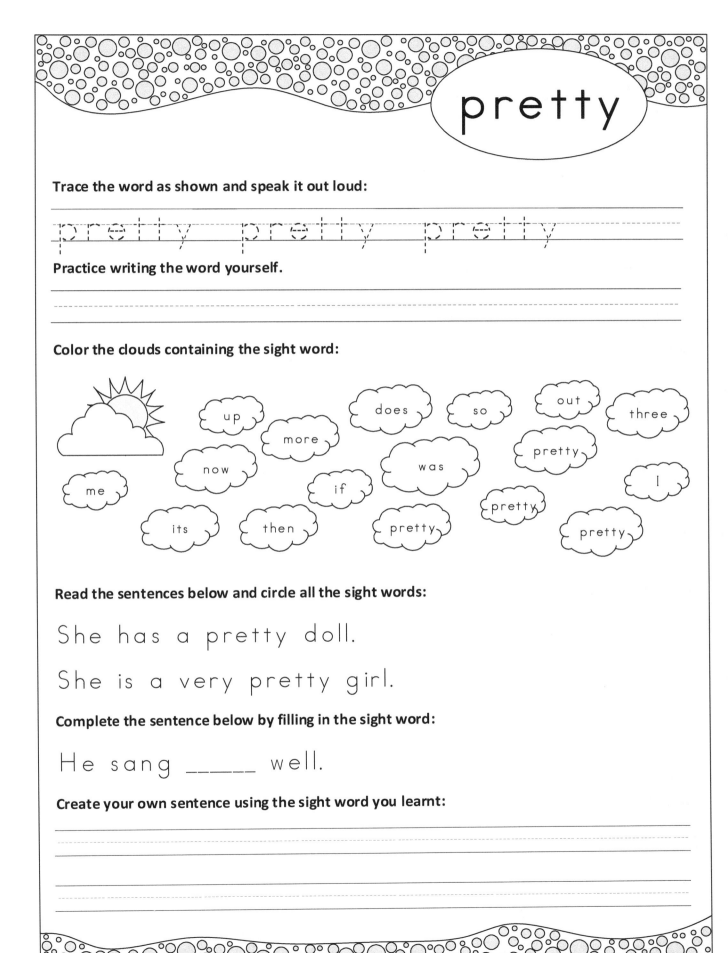

up   does   so   out   three

more

now   was   pretty

me   if   I

its   then   pretty   pretty

pretty

Read the sentences below and circle all the sight words:

She has a pretty doll.

She is a very pretty girl.

Complete the sentence below by filling in the sight word:

He sang _____ well.

Create your own sentence using the sight word you learnt:

one

Trace the word as shown and speak it out loud:

one   one   one   one   one

Practice writing the word yourself.

Color the clouds containing the sight word:

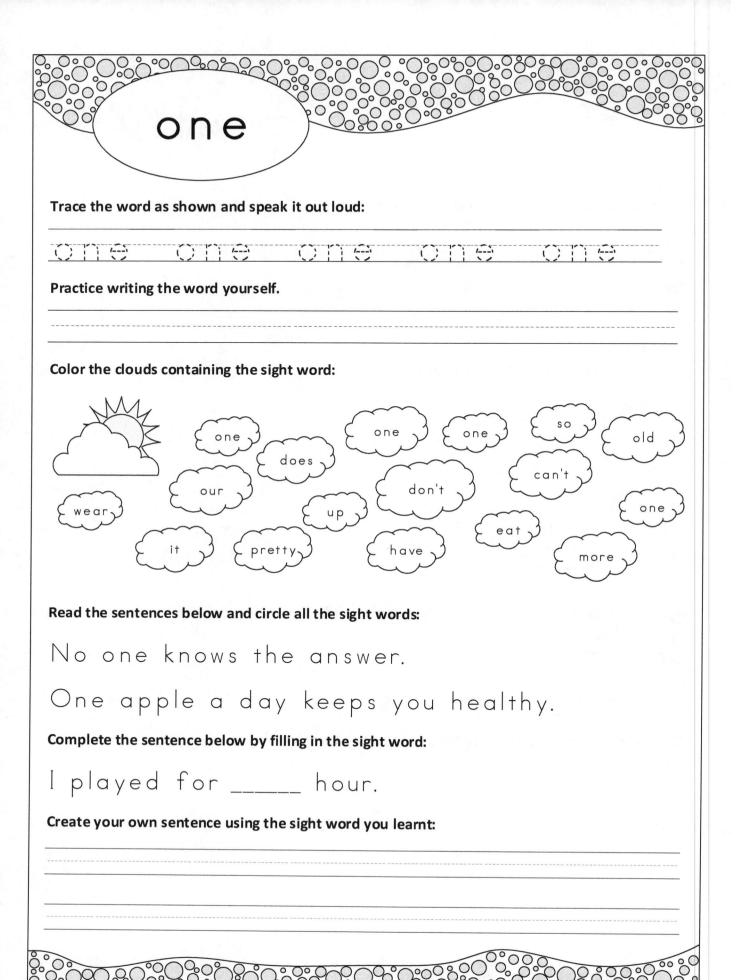

Read the sentences below and circle all the sight words:

No one knows the answer.

One apple a day keeps you healthy.

Complete the sentence below by filling in the sight word:

I played for _____ hour.

Create your own sentence using the sight word you learnt:

put

Trace the word as shown and speak it out loud:

put   put   put   put   put

Practice writing the word yourself.

Color the clouds containing the sight word:

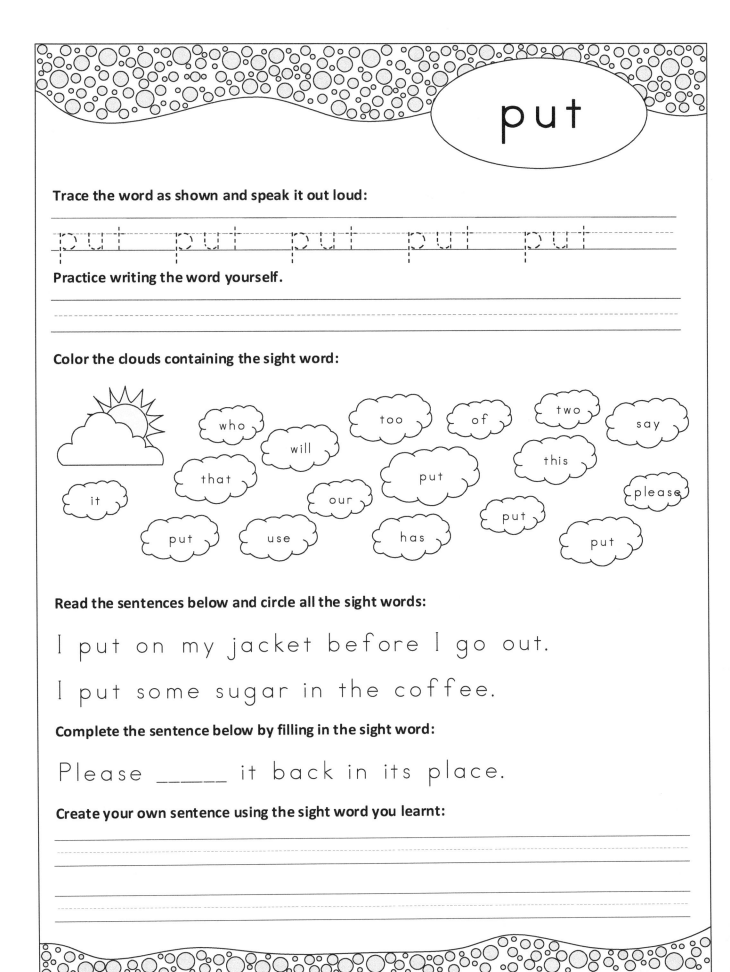

who   will   too   of   two   say
that   put   this
it   our   put   please
put   use   has   put

Read the sentences below and circle all the sight words:

I put on my jacket before I go out.

I put some sugar in the coffee.

Complete the sentence below by filling in the sight word:

Please _____ it back in its place.

Create your own sentence using the sight word you learnt:

want

Trace the word as shown and speak it out loud:

want   want   want   want

Practice writing the word yourself.

Color the clouds containing the sight word:

pretty   if   go   must   or

want

say   want   want   was

wear   want   from

put   old   you   have

Read the sentences below and circle all the sight words:

I want to sleep now.

Do you want a ride?

Complete the sentence below by filling in the sight word:

Take any book you _____

Create your own sentence using the sight word you learnt:

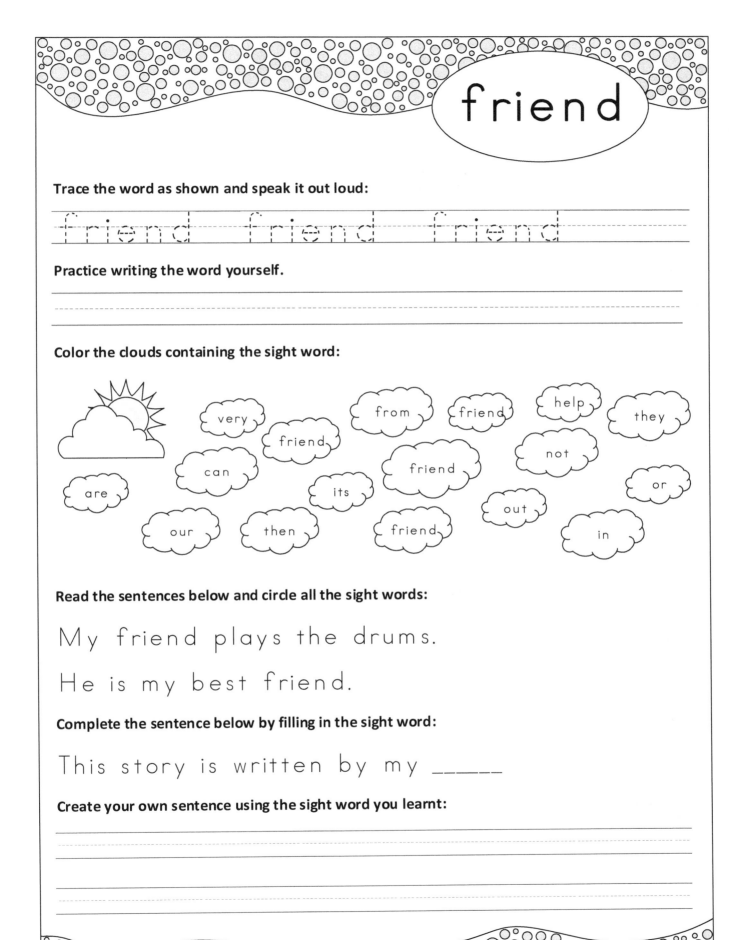

friend

Trace the word as shown and speak it out loud:

friend   friend   friend

Practice writing the word yourself.

Color the clouds containing the sight word:

very   from   friend   help   they

friend   can   friend   not

are   its   out   or

our   then   friend   in

Read the sentences below and circle all the sight words:

My friend plays the drums.

He is my best friend.

Complete the sentence below by filling in the sight word:

This story is written by my _____

Create your own sentence using the sight word you learnt:

with

Trace the word as shown and speak it out loud:

with   with   with   with

Practice writing the word yourself.

Color the clouds containing the sight word:

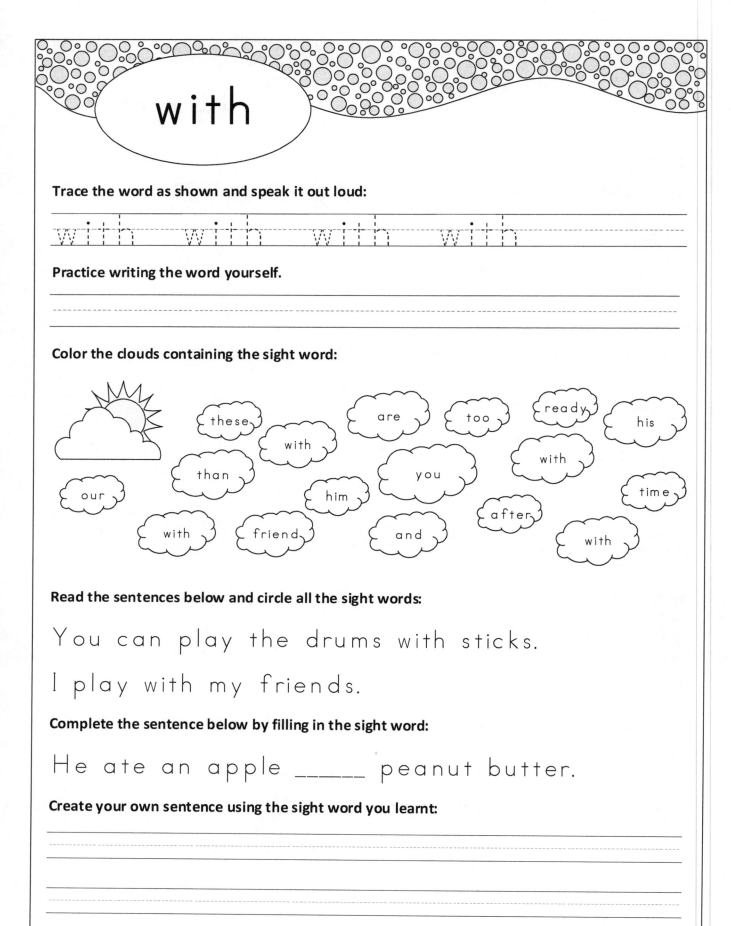

these
with
are
too
ready
his
than
you
with
our
him
time
with
friend
and
after
with

Read the sentences below and circle all the sight words:

You can play the drums with sticks.

I play with my friends.

Complete the sentence below by filling in the sight word:

He ate an apple _____ peanut butter.

Create your own sentence using the sight word you learnt:

the	is	a	on
I	it	too	for
and	if	am	or
so	go	we	his
be	to	who	off

The book is lying **on** the table.	The monkey is eating **a** banana.	The giraffe **is** very tall.	**The** elephant is big.
The bunny called the deer **for** help.	The school is not **too** far.	I am going to try **it** again.	I can read books.
It will rain in a day **or** two.	I **am** good at reading.	I will go even **if** it rains.	The turtle **and** the rabbit are friends.
He cleaned **his** room.	**We** are a happy family.	I **go** to school every day.	He looks **so** tired.
I turned **off** the light.	**Who** left the door open?	I want **to** play in the park.	We should **be** very careful.

up	my	in	he
has	her	do	not
at	an	by	can
you	get	see	of
will	she	him	are

He is my friend.	I play **in** my backyard.	This is **my** school.	Look **up** at the sky.
I am **not** feeling sleepy.	I will **do** the homework.	Her eyes are beautiful.	he **has** a blue car.
Birds **can** fly.	I go to school **by** bus.	The zoo has **an** elephant.	The monkey **at** the zoo looked **at** me.
I have a lot **of** toys.	We **see** with our eyes.	Let us **get** started.	You are smart!
You **are** beautiful!	I will call **him**.	She is my friend.	It **will** snow today.

our	me	old	its
your	but	push	help
when	three	went	that
they	away	must	these
this	live	from	saw

Put the box on **its** side.	This book is **old**.	Gifts make **me** happy.	**Our** house is beautiful.
I need **help** with homework.	**Push** the button to switch the TV on.	I got a pencil, **but** I lost it.	You should share with **your** friends.
I love **that** red car.	I **went** to the park to play.	There were **three** cows in the field.	**When** will it snow?
These books are from the library.	We **must** keep quiet in the library.	The bird flew **away**.	I played with my friends when **they** came.
I **saw** a monkey at the zoo.	He came back **from** school.	I **live** near the school.	Can you help me move **this** desk?

say	those	it's	have
here	don't	like	out
was	does	now	there
time	more	each	were
very	ready	some	than

I **have** many friends.	**It's** going to rain today.	**Those** flowers are beautiful.	Listen carefully to what I **say**.
Let us go **out** and play.	I **like** playing outside.	I **don't** need a new pencil.	I eat **here**, on this table.
The zoo is not far, I want to go **there**.	I have to go to bed **now**.	**Does** he go to school by bus?	It **was** a sunny day.
We **were** quiet in the library.	Brush your teeth after **each** meal.	I don't want any **more** pizza.	It's **time** for bed.
The elephant is bigger **than** the horse.	Give me **some** water.	I am **ready** for school.	Vegetables are **very** good for us.

wear	house	after	ate
where	please	use	own
two	then	eat	jump
what	can't	pretty	one
put	want	friend	with

I **ate** cereal for breakfast.

I went to bed **after** brushing my teeth.

Their **house** is new.

I **wear** a red cap.

I have my **own** room.

I **use** crayons for coloring.

Please come and play with me.

I asked her **where** she was going.

He made the squirrel **jump** off the tree.

I like to **eat** apples.

I ate a burger **then** went for a walk.

I have **two** cats.

One apple a day keeps you healthy.

She has a **pretty** doll.

Penguins **can't** fly.

I don't know **what** to do.

You can play the drums **with** sticks.

My **friend** plays the drums.

I **want** to sleep now.

Please **put** it back in its place.

CPSIA information can be obtained
at www.ICGtesting.com
Printed in the USA
LVHW060344100420
652919LV00015B/959

9 781542 983587